Theatre Games & Activities

Games for building confidence and creativity

Lynda A. Topper

MERIWETHER PUBLISHING LTD.
Colorado Springs, Colorado

Meriwether Publishing Ltd., Publisher
PO Box 7710
Colorado Springs, CO 80933-7710

www.meriwether.com

Editor: Arthur L. Zapel
Associate editor: Audrey Scheck
Cover design: Jan Melvin

© Copyright MMVIII Meriwether Publishing Ltd.
Printed in the United States of America
First Edition

Library of Congress Cataloging-in-Publication Data

Topper, Lynda A.
  Theatre games and activities : games for building confidence and creativity /
  by Lynda A. Topper
    p. cm.
  ISBN 978-1-56608-156-6 (pbk.)
1. Improvisation (Acting) I. Title.
PN2071.I5T67 2008
792.02'8--dc22

                              2008024553

          1   2   3   08   09   10

Table of Contents

Acknowledgments

Many thanks to the family members, friends, former students, and fellow teachers who have generously given me their help and support throughout the years. A special thanks to Arthur Zapel, Editor, for believing in the value of my work, and to Audrey Scheck, Assistant Editor, for being such a pleasure to work with.

Introduction

"I can't get up in front of those people! I just can't!"

How many times have you heard someone say that or perhaps even felt that way yourself? Helping people overcome this common fear is the main goal of this book, and having fun is a strong second.

I am a former teacher of theatre arts and English. I have catalogued many of the materials that I created because I know from personal experience how difficult it is to come up with original, workable ideas day after day. The games and activities contained here can be used by people of a variety of ages and abilities. They can be used in theatre classes, youth groups, camps, adult organizations, and could even provide the basis for an activity-related board game. With a few modifications they can provide hours of entertainment while expanding creativity and communication skills. Even though some people are reluctant to participate at first, after a short while you will see an improved level of confidence. I have been told by students that after completing my course they were able to stand in front of any group for speeches and presentations with minimal anxiety. What a positive benefit this can be to people in both their future work and the challenges of their lifetime.

I have organized the games and activities in a functional way for your convenience. They start simply, with as little stress as possible, and gradually progress to a more challenging level. The order of games may be customized to suit your personal goals and situation.

I hope that what I have compiled here will be helpful to the leader of these activities and rewarding for all participants.

Preface:
How did this book come to be?

About mid-way in my career as a teacher of theatre arts and English, I found myself in a very unexpected situation. I had transferred to a comprehensive public high school with the understanding that I would be teaching only English. Instead I was told that I would have three classes of theatre arts, two classes of English, and would be expected to direct the extracurricular plays. I had very little experience or knowledge of theatre arts.

I found that I was equipped with no money or budget, no books or materials, no curriculum guide, and no during-school auditorium access (it was being used for regular classes due to overcrowding). The result was that I met my three classes of students every day for the entire year of theatre arts in a music room. These courses were electives for which most of the students had signed up to avoid other electives like art and music. In addition, the classes were made up of students ranging in age from 15-19 and in ability from special education (mentally challenged) to gifted and talented (academically advanced). The more advanced theatre arts class was the biggest problem because students had signed up thinking that they would have the previous theatre director and instead got me!

Needless to say it was a very challenging year. I was told that I would not be expected to direct the customary two plays for the first year, but in addition to trying to ride herd on my daily classes I did need to plan a student play for early spring. Thanks to a few non-hostile, sympathetic students, I managed to raise enough money by selling candy to put on a threadbare production of *M*A*S*H*. Without the help of a handful of students and two young long-term substitutes with some theatre experience, I doubt I'd have pulled it off as well as I did. As of spring, I had some money to spend on materials to use with the theatre arts classes and for the production of two after-school plays the next year.

After another year, things began to level off. Two or three things happened that made all the difference. First, I got during-school auditorium access. This gave me a balcony classroom for a base, a coat closet for an office, and a stage and auditorium floor area for games and performances. Secondly, the beginning theatre arts course was changed from a full-year course to a one-semester course. This meant that I could have a more tightly coordinated, successful course for several groups twice a year and the advanced class of students could meet every day of the year. The third thing that helped was a combination of the experience of learning-by-doing and the accumulation of additional materials to further strengthen the curriculum.

Looking back on those years as a teacher of theatre arts and the director of the extracurricular drama program, I can clearly isolate my greatest problem, my greatest satisfaction, and my most memorable experience.

The greatest problem was coming up with original materials and activities for the advanced theatre classes. Remember, these students elected to be there every day (in some cases for three or four years in a row), and they were very eager participants. However, if I dared to repeat any activity, they were not shy about pointing it out immediately. (Actually, they tolerated former activities as long as the topics/assignments were new.) What you see later in this book is a direct result of my efforts to solve that problem.

The greatest satisfaction was seeing some very timid and insecure young people blossom into successful and confident performers.

The most memorable experience was seeing a young man who was mentally challenged blossom as described above. He started the semester shaking all over and unable to make eye contact, and by the end of the term he was happy and confident, able to work with any and all members of his class. At the end of the course, he was unanimously selected by the class for the Best Overall Drama Award, and I will never forget the look on his face when he found out!

Chapter 1
The Planning Process

Analyzing Your Group

A lot of what you will do will depend on the people with whom you are working. If you will be teaching a course, it would be nice to have an idea of the overall ages and ability levels of your students. Very likely you will be dealing with a wide variety, a very heterogeneous group. This can be challenging, but it can also be very refreshing — especially if most of the students are meeting for the first time. If, on the other hand, you are in charge of a youth or adult group that is less diversified, you will need to take that into consideration. If the participants already know one another, you may be faced with good or bad existing relationships. Take this in stride and plan accordingly. The key to the whole issue is grouping. I can't stress enough that you need to be firm in this process in order to ensure that the participants are not allowed to gravitate into cliques.

Evaluating Your Meeting Area

Now that you have analyzed your group, where will you be meeting? From my experience, there are only a few absolute requirements. You will need a space large enough to hold everyone with adequate room for dividing the group into pairs or small groups for short planning sessions. There must be enough space between these clusters so that their business can be accomplished. There must be a performance area, but that can be the same space that was previously used for a planning area. If you have an upraised area or stage, all the better, but this is not absolutely necessary. It is best if everyone is within sight. With young people especially, not knowing where they are or what they're doing can be troublesome. Better to be safe than sorry.

The only other requirement is that you have lots of folding chairs — a versatile tool! You should have at least ten more chairs than the number of participants (including you). Try to avoid using an area where there is a lot of other furniture.

Setting Appropriate Objectives

Now that you know more about your group and space, what do you plan to accomplish? You want them to have fun, but they need to accomplish something as well. The games and activities in this book are organized from simple and less stressful to more complex and challenging.

When I taught theatre arts, I posted a daily attainable objective. I had each student copy it at the beginning of the session into his theatre arts journal. At the end of each session, students were to briefly describe what it was they accomplished that day and how they felt about it. This journal was used as a part of my evaluation process for the course. You can determine whether or not this will work for you, but I strongly suggest that you post a daily objective and, at the very least, have a verbal discussion of how the objective was met at the end of each session. I've provided objectives for most of the activities; if these suit your purposes, use them. If you have other goals to accomplish, set them now.

Begin the course with two simple objectives. The first should be to get acquainted, and the second should be to get acclimated. Begin gently to deal with students' fear of facing the group. It may be that your group is already acquainted, but you can still use an activity that bypasses the basic identification portion and uses some other get-to-know-you topics.

Organizing Your Materials around Your Objectives

If you are a beginner, you can follow my sequence of activities and objectives. There is room to pick and choose as you go along, but I suggest you keep some kind of record of what you use, when, and with whom. I hope you can find a way to incorporate some of these games and activities into your own curriculum. You will notice that some of the activities, like "Charades" and "Mirrors," are traditional theatre games. You can put a new spin on them when you use them to suit specific purposes. In addition, don't forget to incorporate other media where possible. If you are doing pantomime, for instance, and can show a good mime performance as an example, all the better. There are good films and DVDs available on appropriate issues. How about a field trip to see a live performance? It never hurts to supplement for the sake of variety, but be forewarned — your little "hams" much prefer to be involved themselves rather than watch others!

Deciding on Methods to Assess Achievement and Reward Progress

The last stage of getting started involves follow-up. Obviously the big question is whether this will be a graded or non-graded activity. Even if no grade is to be assigned, the participants will get much more out of the experience if they can clearly see what they have accomplished.

When I taught theatre arts, I had groups with an age range of five years and a range of abilities from one end of the spectrum to the other. I had to come up with a satisfactory and fair way to judge these young people. First, I had to consider attendance. After all, how can someone participate who isn't there? In my case, my school had an unexcused absence policy. As a result, a student could (and occasionally did) fail the course simply by not attending enough. Next, I considered participation. Although this is somewhat subjective, it basically boils down to, "Did Johnny try to do what was asked of him each session or not?" Then there was the completion of the daily journal. This could not be judged academically. The requirement was to copy the daily objective each day and record a brief summary of what was accomplished and the student's personal reaction to it. The journal was judged simply on how many of the required entries were made and how many of the handouts were included. I provided a checklist of what should be in the journals before I collected them. The final thing considered in the grade was an exam that was a requirement at my school. My exam included a written portion and a performance portion. The written part was not judged by academic standards and focused on what had been done throughout the course (see Chapter 10 for more information). The performances were graded with the understanding of how far the individual had progressed during the course in relation to his age and ability level. Most of the grades were "good" or "excellent," but with certain standards to meet, the students knew better than to think they were being given a free ride.

Even if no grade is involved, there are some things you should do to make the sessions more meaningful. One simple practice is to encourage and expect polite applause to follow every performance, regardless of length and quality. If participants regularly announce the end of their performance by stating the word "curtain," this becomes a clear signal to the audience for applause. Most students followed my lead without a problem, and this simple act became a reward that encouraged continued achievement.

Another technique is to periodically require the audience to do a simple evaluation (written, oral, or both). Peer- and/or self-evaluations work well, too, especially when followed with discussion. Examine any written evaluations before sharing them with the group. The last thing you want is for negative or spiteful comments to undermine the dynamics of the group.

Another non-graded possibility is to invite an audience from outside of the class. Even without written feedback, this provides the performers with audience reaction that is usually positive.

Chapter 2
The Challenge of the First Meeting

Setting Up the Meeting Area

Before your first session, you will need to be sure that the area is clearly established (at least for the first few activities). After that, the group members can pitch in when rearrangement is needed. Be sure to know what needs to be done prior to an activity and keep your instructions clear to avoid confusion.

Since the first activity in my sequence builds from a basic circle, I suggest you set up a circle of folding chairs facing inward to accommodate all of the participants and yourself. When students arrive, they can sit in any available chairs. From your seat in the circle you can go over the basic rules, regulations, and goals before you start; get activity-oriented ASAP.

I will provide specific suggestions about the arrangement of the meeting place throughout the games and activities, but for the most part a basic circle or single line of chairs will be the starting point. After assignments are given from this starting point and the pairs or groups are sent to other areas to plan, they should return to their original seats until called on to perform. If space allows, you can use an opening in the circle (making a kind of horseshoe) for your performance area. If you have a stage or upraised platform for the performances, then a single line of chairs is preferable. One way to decide when to start the performances (and end the planning time) is to have the pairs or groups return to their original seats when finished. As soon as most everyone is back, issue a verbal time-check to those still planning, and you should be underway quickly. By having students return to their original chairs, you will feel more comfortable about asking them to leave personal items/valuables there. The items are in sight during the planning and performance stages and near their owners while they are in the audience.

A brief note about the essential, versatile folding chairs: You will find that in addition to being useful as chairs, they can also be used to represent everything from walls to tables to cars. They can be a source of amazing creativity and imagination.

Grouping Techniques

Whether your students are acquainted with one another or not, they will bring with them certain preconceived notions (and possibly prejudices) about their classmates. This will be true in all groups, but it

8

can be especially destructive with adolescents. Rule #1: *Never* (OK, almost never) allow participants to select their own partners or group members! There are a few activities in this book with which you may disregard this rule, but not many. You want students to intermingle so quickly and so often that they learn not to even ask to work with a specific person.

How do you do this? The simplest way is using numbers and/or letters. If I was going to work with pairs, I would point to one student at a time, alternating between one end of the group and the other, and send pairs immediately to a planning area with an assignment. In that case, no numbers or letters are needed, but you have avoided selecting those sitting next to their buddies as partners. If I needed to split the group in half, I would assign everyone numbers in sequence and then send the evens to one area and the odds to another. Other groupings depend on how many would work best in each group and how many participants you have all together. If there are 25 students and you think 5 per group would be desirable, then point and number or letter accordingly: 1-5 or A-E with 1s (A's) going here, 2s (B's) going there, and so on. These numbers and letters will also prove useful when you are calling for performances. Simply call the numbers/letters in the order in which they were assigned. This saves time, begins with those who had the most planning time, and avoids missing anyone. Since you will often have the groups seated or standing in a line or circle to begin, these methods should not be too time consuming or difficult to accomplish, and you will succeed at the first goal of grouping: Keep it random!

To efficiently and quickly give out assignments, you might simply walk to a group's meeting area and verbally give the group its assignment. This works best if there are four or fewer large groups. An alternative for this situation is to tell one member of each group the assignment and have him communicate it to his other group members. In either case, be sure to check back with each group at least once during planning to answer questions and offer suggestions.

For all other grouping situations, I would suggest using cards. When I directed after-school plays, I always had lots of leftover tickets that were blank on one side and just the right size for writing down assignments. (Index cards would work well, too.) Write the assignments on the cards and have a representative from each group draw one card (sight-unseen) from the deck. This keeps you from being accused of favoritism or partiality. It is a quick, easy, and democratic system.

Be sure to collect and save the cards after each activity for future use. Keep them organized; keep each deck together with a rubber band

and label each deck with details such as when and where it was used. Be sure to include on the label any comments about the success or failure of the activity.

Am I Now Ready to Initiate the Action?

Let's face it — there are always variables. However, if you have done all (or most) of the planning and preparation I've suggested, you are ready! Remember to make your goals and objectives clear to your students. Clarify any rules or regulations that apply to the activities. Be friendly but firm (you must be in charge). Watch your timing; you know when you will have to stop. Leave at least five minutes at the end of each session for everyone to return to his original place for some quiet assessment and evaluation time. You might ask a few harmless questions like "What did you particularly enjoy doing today? Why?" "What performance stood out in your mind as being particularly good today? Why?" and "What do you think you learned today?" This time of reflection at the end of the session provides stability after what can be a very active and stimulating experience. Don't forget to follow up on the posted daily objective.

Chapter 3
Getting Acquainted and Acclimated

I mentioned that I have organized the games and activities from the simplest and least stressful to the more challenging. You will want your participants to get used to working with one another and standing in front of the group as quickly and as gently as possible. I suggest you start with a game I call:

Circle Rotation

Objective: Students will be able to meet their fellow participants and learn a little bit about most of them.

Arrange one circle of chairs facing in and another circle facing out so that pairs of participants sit face to face. Explain to the participants that when you call out "Rotate," the outer circle should stand and move in a clockwise direction to sit facing another person. Depending on the number of participants, there may be one empty chair. You will stand outside of the circle to direct and observe during this activity, so point out that the un-partnered person will have a brief break as the rotation proceeds.

Now you are ready to begin. Your first direction will be, "Introduce yourself to your partner and give your age, grade, etc. Then each of you will tell the other one fact about yourself related to the category I give you."

Give them the first category (see page 12), and allow a few minutes for this process to take place. It is not necessary to wait until all of them are finished talking. Keep it moving! When ready, call out "Rotate" and give a new category. The people in the outer circle will then move to the next partner and proceed immediately to share information.

Continue repeating these steps until the students have made one complete rotation. Since this initial procedure will only introduce half of the group, you will need to proceed as follows: Have the people in the outer circle re-form in another area with pairs of chairs facing each other as before (this can be random). Then have every other person in the inner circle move his chair to face the person to his right. Now you have two sets of smaller rotation circles. Follow the same procedure as before, having both of the outer circles rotate as you direct. Make a complete rotation and stop. Most (if not all) of your subjects should have met now.

Examples of Categories

Family
Pets
School
Hobbies
Likes
Dislikes
Sports

Depending on how much time you have, you might continue in these two circles and play "Question Rotation" (see below). If you would like a follow-up to this activity, you might meet again in one large circle and have volunteers offer bits of information that they have learned about other participants. If your group was already acquainted, you might skip the name/identification part of the activity and just have participants share facts in each category.

Question Rotation

Use the same double circle set up as in Circle Rotation.

Examples of Topic Questions

What was your first day at school like? What do you wish it had been like?

What was your summer like? What do you wish your summer had been like?

What do you look forward to most this year? What do you look forward to least?

Now that your participants have met (or become better acquainted), it is time to add a bit of movement and acclimate them to the performance area (PA).

Stage Walk-Up

Objective: Students will be able to briefly introduce and provide a little more information about themselves to the rest of the group from the performance area.

Start out standing in one large horseshoe formaton facing inward. If you have a stage or upraised platform, start instead in one straight line facing the stage. Hand out cards to each participant (list follows). When ready, have one person walk to the PA, state his name, age, and grade, read his card (filling in the blanks), and finish by saying "curtain."

For this activity, make sure that the next person to perform stands and moves into the PA during the applause for the first person. If you are using a stage, assign a walk-up side and a walk-down side to save time and avoid collisions. Repeat this process until everyone has performed. If more time is still available, have the cards passed to different people and repeat the procedure.

Statements for Cards

My favorite weekday is _____ because _____.

My favorite song or type of music is _____ because _____.

My relatives are unlike most people's because they _____.

Over the summer, the happiest day I spent was _____ because _____.

My favorite color is _____ because _____.

If I was going to go to the moon for a year, I would take _____ because _____.

What I like least about school is _____ because _____.

As far as personal opinions go, I feel most strongly about _____ because _____.

When I get depressed and want to cheer up, I _____ because _____.

What I like most about being my age is _____ because _____.

When I read a newspaper, the section I go to first is _____ because _____.

If my father/mother was asked to describe me, he/she would say _____ because _____.

The biggest problem with the world is _____ because _____.

If I could travel back in time, I would choose to go to _____ because _____.

If I had to quit school today and go to work, I would _____ because _____.

The quality I like most in a teacher is _____ because _____.

I took this course because _____.

The thing that makes me the most angry is _____ because _____.

If I could change one thing about myself, it would be _____ because _____.

Weekends get on my nerves when _____ because _____.

When someone compliments me, it usually is about _____ because _____.

The member of my family with whom I am closest is _____ because _____.

The performer I would most like to meet is _____ because _____.

If I picked one thing to accomplish this year, it would be _____ because _____.

The TV role that I'd most like to play is _____ because _____.

The time in my life I was most afraid was _____ because _____.

If I could travel anywhere in the world it would be _____ because _____.

A pet I've had or would like to have is _____ because _____.

The thing I remember most about last year is _____ because _____.

The trait I most admire in people is _____ because _____.

Chapter 4
Nonverbal Group Activities

Now that your group has been introduced and acclimated, it is time to start working on acting without speech. Point out to the group that in order to be a good actor, you first need to learn to communicate without using words. Remind them that we all pick up on and react to body language before we speak to someone. Sometimes we even pre-judge others before we know them. This group of sessions will help you to improve these skills.

Note: Don't forget to incorporate other media in this section. Use old silent movies, films of mime and clown performances, etc. Contemporary Drama Service (www.contemporarydrama.com) has many excellent clown and mime DVDs.

Since we are just starting, we will go with the safety-in-numbers theory. It should be a lot easier for our novice participants to perform for the first time if they're working with others.

Line Games

Objective: Students will be able to pantomime individual topics directed by the leader while standing among a large group.

Use the following games over a number of sessions. The objective remains the same; only the topics called out by the leader will vary. After exposure to pantomiming as a part of a large group, the participants should feel more comfortable about the experience in general.

For each of the following activities, the group will be divided in half. Start with a single line of chairs in front of a wide performance area. Divide the participants into two groups. Have first group leave their seats (and any belongings) and form a line in the PA facing the audience. Have them spread out by extending both arms until they are unable to touch anyone near them.

Word Lists

The performing line must respond non-verbally to lists of random words called out by the teacher. They will react individually to the words, not as a group. Each person in line must respond in some way. Groups exchange places and the process is repeated.

Sample Word List

Watermelon	Birds	Vacation
Errors	Telephone	Candy
Kleenex	Sunshine	Stripes
Art	Aluminum foil	Ring
Bench	Tuna fish	America
Supper	Video	Shampoo
Can	Crutches	Diet
Lavatory	Assignment	Janitor
Surprise		

Additional Word Lists

1. Ground hog, peanuts and popcorn, blue-green, phone, man and woman, doorway, locks and keys, etc.
2. Fruit juice, hallways, hot pink, curly hair, teenager, hands and arms, hot car, ice cold, sweater weather, electric charge, wheels rolling, children at play, college, time, toasted marshmallows, writer's cramp, trash collection, fun and games, letters home, nurse, etc.
3. Pumpkins, junkyard, food fight, disaster, bubbles, long hair, lawn mower, senior prom, pregnancy, pocketbook, grocery store, watches and clocks, blond and beautiful, sunburned, fresh air, red, testing, birds and bees, color of money, academy awards, the lottery, paradise, purple rain, report cards, etc.

Line Rolls

This activity is the same as "Word Lists" above, but the emphasis in the words is emotional rather than completely random.

Sample Word Lists

1. Dark, cold, musty, alone, fearful, trouble, scream, hurry, crash, fall, hurt, cry, light, relieve, call, voice, louder, trust, safety, etc.
2. Rain, bark, tree, grow, tall, spring, birds, nest, eggs, warm, blue, clear, sun, enjoy, walk, run, play, laugh, share, friends, help, blend, relax, trust, happy, etc.

Line Pantomimes

The teacher calls out various activities which must be pantomimed in line by half the class at a time.

Sample Activity Lists

General Activities: Painting a picture, mowing the lawn, adjusting the TV, finding a book from the library shelf, removing a sliver from a finger, etc.

Sports: Bowling, tennis, football, hockey, fishing, track, baseball, basketball, etc.

Eating Foods: Cotton candy, banana, apple, ice cream cone, crab legs, lemon, peanuts, etc.

Animals: Horse, monkey, frog, snake, cat, lion, alligator, skunk, etc.

Emotions: Fear, pity, hatred, love, suspicion, sadness, anxiety, sympathy, etc.

Large-Group Pantomimes

Reflections (a spin–off of Mirrors)

Objective: Students will be able to physically reflect the actions of various group members as closely as possible as directed by the leader.

This is a fun game, but it requires a large space and some flexibility. Meet your group in the middle of the area, leaving as much open space as possible around the outside. Divide them into two groups: ones and twos. Have 1s leave their seats and place themselves standing around the outer walls facing inward. After they are in place, send the twos to stand facing the ones, forming pairs. Tell them that the twos will be rotators while the ones will remain in place. You will stand somewhere in the middle, observing and calling out commands.

Call out a leader and a type of movement (see lists on page 18).

Note: Each time a new pair is formed, allow both participants a chance to be the leader, starting with the one who meets the leader command first.

Call out the following commands to be followed by each pair. The leader will initiate the movement in slow motion, and the partner will attempt to reflect the leader's movements as accurately as possible.

Commands

"Go" or "begin" to initiate action
"Freeze" to stop action in progress
"Relax" to unfreeze
"Rotate" to move rotators to their next partner

Note: Verbal comments can be made during the activity by the instructor to encourage performance. The biggest problems result from leaders who move too quickly.

Proceed with the activity until one full rotation has been completed. If time allows, or a second session of this activity is desired, simply re-group in a random manner and repeat.

Suggested Leader Commands

Tallest	Shortest
Darkest hair	Lightest hair
Darkest shirt	Lightest shirt
Darkest shoes	Lightest shoes
Most colorful clothing	Least colorful clothing
Youngest	Oldest
Shortest hair	Longest hair
Largest foot	Smallest foot
Most jewelry	Least jewelry

Suggested Movement Commands

Hands and arms	Feet and legs
Twists and bends	Exercises
Swimming	Shaving face or legs
Putting on makeup	Brushing teeth
Dancing	Boxing
Muscle poses	Getting dressed
Fixing your hair	Jogging
Jumping rope	Washing a window/mirror
Writing on a board	

Charades

Objective: Students will be able to act out the titles of various movies, songs, books, and TV shows without the use of words.

As the instructor, you will have to supply some background on the use of hand signals before beginning this game. You will also need a stopwatch or timing device to indicate the amount of time used. Designate a timekeeper and a scorekeeper so that you can concentrate on other tasks. Prepare cards with titles of movies, TV shows, books, and songs. (If desired you can have each group make up the cards to be used by the opposing group. Use caution, however, to avoid inappropriate choices.) You will be the one to verify that the correct answer is achieved.

Note: Since this activity is fairly well known, a lot of details will not be provided here. As a general review, no words/sounds can be used, no writing or drawing is allowed, and some readily accepted hand motions are normally known and used.

Divide into two groups. Have one group sit together on one side of the room and the other on the opposite side, both facing the PA. Start with the person on the far end of the ones. Have him draw a card from your deck, give a signal to start, and stop when correct answer is given or time is up (usually two minutes).

Tabulate the score and announce the winning team at the end. The winner will have used the least amount of time. Repeat the activity at another session if all the participants did not get a chance to perform. Keep the cards that were used separate from the others to avoid repetition.

Variation

If desired, the same beginning procedure can be followed but with a change in the manner of communication. If a large chalkboard or dry-erase board is available, participants can draw to communicate. As in traditional Charades, no words or letters may be written.

Suggested Titles for Category Cards

Movies: *Meet Me in St. Louis, Casablanca, ET,* etc.
Songs: "People," "Poison Ivy," "Release Me," etc.
Books: *Green Eggs and Ham, the Bible, Mommy Dearest,* etc.
TV shows: *All in the Family, The Cosby Show, I Love Lucy,* etc.

Freeze Scenes

Objective: As members of a large group, students will be able to play a part in communicating a general topic.

This activity requires a setup similar to the last activity. Have the topics on cards to be drawn as usual.

Form two large groups. Send one group to the performance area, and the other to the audience area.

Give a general topic to the performing group and provide time for them to select a specific scene and form a "freeze scene" which suggests/depicts the topic without movement. While the performing group is planning and arranging, have the audience face away from the performance area. They may turn back around only when told.

When the performing group is ready, reveal the freeze scene to the audience and have them guess what is depicted.

Note: If a very specific answer is desired, the general category should be revealed. If only the general category is desired, no prompting should be necessary. For example, if the general topic is "Current national event," and that is the desired response to be guessed by the audience, no prompting may be necessary. However, if the desired response is a specific national event, such as the launch of the space shuttle, the audience may be told ahead of time that the scene depicts a current national event.

Continue this process, switching the performance and audience groups, until time is up or all the topics are used.

Suggested General Topics

Current national event	School event
Scene from a familiar book	Scene from a familiar movie
Controversial issue	Ethnic holiday
Religious event	Patriotic event
Famous sports event	Famous landmark
Famous theme park	Exotic location
Scene from a famous song	Well-known entertainer
Advertisement	

Musical Games

Move to the Music

Objective: Students will be able to individually move to music they have not heard in advance while in the company of a group of their classmates.

Gather a selection of music with a variety of tempos.

Form two groups of participants. Send one group to the performance area, and have the other group situated as the audience.

When the music is playing, each performing participant must move to the music in some manner. When the music stops, each must freeze in position until it starts again.

Have the two groups change places and repeat the procedure as many times as desired.

Note: Students should be aware that they do not have to dance in this activity. Any appropriate movements are acceptable (exercising, twisting/bending, etc.) as long as they are in time with the tempo of the music. Allowing participants to form pairs or groups spontaneously is up to the instructor and should be clarified prior to beginning the activity.

Music Grab Bag

Objective: Students will be able to work as a part of a group to perform in some way to a randomly selected piece of music.

Gather a variety of music on separate CDs and place the CDs in a large, covered container.

Divide participants into two large groups and send each to an area already equipped with music players. These areas should ideally be isolated from each other, but if complete isolation is not an option, separate the groups as much as possible and instruct them to keep the volume down.

A student in each group should draw a CD from the container sight unseen, and the groups should be given time to select a song (or part of a song) and plan a performance to do with the song.

When planning time is up, both groups will perform. This can be done in a separate area with separate equipment if available, or one of the two group planning areas can be used.

Notes: Be sure that selections are firm. Do not allow trade-ins or substitutions. It is not important (nor desirable) that the performance involve the entire piece, only a representative portion.

If you use commercially produced CDs rather than ones you make yourself, they should be labeled to clarify which tracks may be used. Providing too many choices will just cause confusion and defeat the goal of the activity.

Every member of the group must participate in some way in the performance in order to receive credit.

Performance Suggestions

Imitate the original performers

Move to the music

Act out the lyrics/story

Complete activities appropriate to the musical background (dance contest, fashion show, etc.)

Small-Group Pantomimes

Machines

Objective: Students will be able to work as part of a group to visually represent a variety of machines.

For this activity, form groups of five or six. After explaining the basic procedure, send each group to a designated area for planning with an assignment. Check in with each group at least once to answer questions and offer suggestions as needed.

You may choose to have the audience cluster in a standing position around the performing group since the performances will be relatively short.

When finished with the first set (Real), proceed to the second (Fantasy). Or, better yet, do more of the real machines to warm up for the more challenging fantasy machines.

Real

Groups are told to create a working appliance (toaster, blender, can opener, etc.) and given an appropriate amount of time to prepare before presentation. Observers are allowed to guess the appliance, but only after the presentation is complete.

Fantasy

Groups are formed and one person in each group starts a movement. A second person assumes a position which allows him to come in contact with the first person and begin a corresponding motion.

Each remaining person in the group does the same in turn, making sure that the last person makes contact in some way with the very first. When performing, groups can be instructed to go faster, slower, or to freeze at the call of the leader.

Fairy Tales/Other Narratives

Objective: Students will be able to work as part of a group to relate stories of some kind in pantomime.

Form groups of five or six. After reviewing the basic idea, send the groups to planning areas with their assignments. Groups meet to verbally review famous stories, decide on parts, placement, etc. When ready, call on groups in order that they were assigned to perform. In the case of the first set (Fairy Tales), the story portrayed is usually pretty obvious, but ask for a show of hands to guess anyway.

Once they've warmed up with familiar stories, go on to the second set (Other Narratives), which is more subjective and challenging. Be flexible when accepting guesses about what is being portrayed by the performances. You or the performance group may decide when the guess is close enough.

Note: All must participate, but some may be objects rather than people. Also, some may assume more than one role if needed.

Fairy Tales

"Snow White"
"Goldilocks and the Three Bears"
"Hansel and Gretel"
"Cinderella"
"Rapunzel"
"Rumpelstiltskin"

"The Three Little Pigs"
"Jack and the Beanstalk"
"Little Red Riding Hood"
"Sleeping Beauty"
"Little Miss Muffet"

Note: There are many versions of these stories, so encourage participants to be creative. In some cases variations will prove advantageous. For instance, there could be more bears in "Goldilocks," Cinderella could become Cinderfella, Snow White could become Snow Black, etc.

Other Narratives

Famous movies
Local (perhaps school) events

Historical events
Current/famous TV shows

23

Suggestion for assigning narratives: Verbally announce the general topic (movies, current events, etc.) to every group at once. Each group should consult on which movie/event they would like to do and then send a representative to inform you of their decision. If more than one group chooses the same movie/event, assignments should be based on a first-come, first-serve situation. This procedure encourages quick thinking and eliminates discontent about what is assigned.

Sensory Activities

Blind Trust

Objective: Students will be able to work with partners to alternately experience a portion of time when they are deprived of their sense of sight and therefore are reliant on the use of their other senses.

Notes: This is an activity that requires caution! You are responsible for the safety of the members of your group, so make the rules very clear to everyone before you start. This is also one of the rare times when random grouping is not encouraged. Pairing by choice is preferred because of the level of trust that is required. By this point, the students should be fairly comfortable with one another. Any un-paired person should work as your assistant by circulating among the pairs to ensure safety and compliance with the rules.

You can start with either a line or a circle since there will not be any PA needed.

This activity is basically nonverbal, however, some communication will occur. While this can be a very rewarding experience, it should not be undertaken without caution (particularly when young people are involved).

Form pairs of students who are reasonably comfortable with each other.

One member of each pair is blindfolded. (Clean sheets cut into strips make effective, inexpensive blindfolds which can be easily laundered for reuse.) After directions (and cautions) are given by the teacher, the sighted member leads the blindfolded member on a walk around the designated area.

On a visual signal from the teacher, sighted members lead blindfolded members to a seat and then move away from them. When all blindfolded members are seated, all talking ceases.

After a period of silence (during which participants experience the disorientation that results from a loss of senses) the teacher will ask each

24

blindfolded member to describe his experiences and feelings.

When directed, blindfolds are removed and placed on the other member of each pair; the process is repeated.

Caution: The success of this activity is largely dependent on the cooperation and maturity of the participants. Obviously there is opportunity for injury to occur. However, with proper precaution this activity can allow participants to experience sensory deprivation and its resulting dependence. Usually the result is a greater appreciation and awareness of our senses.

Sensory Passing

Objective: Students will be able to apply the use of their senses (other than sight) to experience a variety of objects.

This activity involves the entire group and requires a tight enough circle that participants can pass objects easily without being able to see. There will naturally be reactions to the handling of some items, so make your rules clear before beginning. Remember that this is a nonverbal activity (no speaking is allowed). You should remain standing outside of the circle to observe, give directions, and correct behavior as necessary.

Form a large circle where the chairs are within easy arm's reach of one another. Have all participants seated in the chairs and blindfolded.

Hand each participant a sensory object and allow several minutes for non-visual examination.

At an appropriate time, say "pass." Participants will hand their objects to the person to their left. Several minutes will be allotted for examination before "pass" is called again and the procedure continues. Continue this passing procedure until objects return to their original locations.

Notes: Blindfolds should not be removed until directed by the leader. Care should be taken when handling and passing objects to avoid damage. Dropping, throwing, or discussing the objects is prohibited. While some verbal reaction is to be expected, communication should be minimal.

Conclusion to the activity: The person (still blindfolded) holding his original object should verbalize to the others what he thinks he is holding and why. Others may comment if they remember experiencing the object in the passing. Students will be forced to rely on senses other than sight to guess what they are holding.

Suggested Sensory Objects
Fruits
Vegetables
Natural items from the outdoors (bark, moss, etc.)

Try to select things which have a strong sensory appeal but are not all obvious. Things with unusual texture, shape, and smell tend to provide the best results.

Chapter 5
Nonverbal Individual Activities

Object Pantomimes
Objective: Students will be able to individually pantomime the use or handling of objects.

Have the group seated with you in a circle. List (on cards) a wide variety of objects. Assign one to each participant.

Have the subject at one point in the circle stand in place to pantomime the object on the card selected. The subject opposite him will try and identify the object when the pantomime is complete. If there is a problem with the identification, ask for a show of hands until someone guesses correctly.

This is the first time for individual performances, so remember to use the word "curtain" at the end of each performance followed by applause prior to the identification. Do at least one round of relatively simple objects followed by a round of more difficult objects.

Suggested Objects
Simple: Stethoscope, can opener, etc.
More difficult: Calendar, horoscope, bank vault, cemetery, windmill, etc.

Occupation Pantomimes
Objective: Students will be able to individually pantomime various occupations.

Follow the same procedure as in "Object Pantomimes," using occupations instead of objects.

Suggested Occupations
Truant officer	Programmer
Scientist	Survey taker
Poet	Athlete
Chauffeur	Lawyer
Banker	

Pantomimes From Script or Source

Objective: Students will be able to individually pantomime an activity that represents a short piece of writing they have read.

Use the circle approach as in previous pantomimes. Prepare cards with selections like familiar poems, song lyrics, fables, etc., for use. Keep the selections short, simple, and fairly recognizable (especially if you are working with subjects of limited ability).

After each subject draws a card from the deck, allow planning time for them to read the selections silently and prepare.

Have performances when ready. The audience may give suggestions post-performance. Remember to reward participants with applause after each curtain.

The performers may read their selections as a conclusion to the activity.

Unusual Pantomimes

Objective: Students will be able to individually pantomime common activities in unusual locations or situations.

Use the same circle setup as before, distributing cards with assignments. Have a show of hands to identify topics.

Participants are given a common activity (such as walking) and then an unusual location or situation in which they might be doing it.

Unusual Locations

Through a forest of man-eating plants
Over a ravine full of crocodiles
Down a road of sticky tar
Through a dark, dangerous alley
Through the burning desert looking for water
In outer space
Across a wide street on a windy night

Freeze Scene Pantomimes

Objective: Students will be able to individually freeze in a position which represents a certain topic or category.

Use the same procedure as before with rotating performances and show-of-hand identification.

Assign each person a topic. When called upon, the person should assume a frozen position which illustrates the topic and hold that position until someone guesses correctly.

Notes: You will decide when guesses are close enough to be correct. If no one guesses correctly in a reasonable period of time, reveal the topic and move on to the next performance. The person who guesses correctly can select the next performer.

Suggested Topics

Occupation	Specific animal
Sport	Vehicle
Amusement ride	Toy
Type of weather/season	Specific machine
Fairy tale character	Household chore
Family member	Room
Food	Daily activity

Musical Pantomimes

Objective: Students will be able to individually pantomime to a short piece of music that they have pre-selected.

Students are given the following assignment with time to prepare and a date of presentation.

Assignment

Select a song on tape, CD, etc., and plan a pantomime to be performed during the entire song or a select portion of it. You may use others in the performance to help you, but only you will get credit for the selection, planning, creativity, etc. Use of costumes and props is optional but will obviously enhance the end product. Be sure to have your musical selection set at the appropriate place prior to the performance.

Pantomime Suggestions
Lip sync
Act out lyrics
Dance or move to the music
Complete an activity which has something to do with the song
Use props/costumes that relate to the song in some way

Notes: This activity requires pre-planning but can be a lot of fun. Decide what form of music you will use (CD, tape, other) and assign dates for the presentations. It is not necessary to require the use of an entire selection, but a significant portion is expected. Use a straight line in front of the PA as a setup. To be fair about deciding who performs when, write the names of all participants on cards. Have the students draw (sight unseen) from the deck. The name drawn performs first. Then draw again for second, third, etc. This way you'll be sure not to miss anyone.

Do not allow any negative comments or inappropriate laughter to undermine this activity. Provide lots of encouraging applause to reward every performance.

It is up to you whether you allow the provider of the music to use other group members as part of the performance. If this is allowed, make it clear that the additional group members are only to act as extras to the main performer. If working with young people, be sure to require G-rated music selections to avoid embarrassment or criticism.

Mime
Objective: Students will be able to perform an individual mime routine as a follow-up to viewing examples of this type.

If you have access to media examples of mime, show them first. Follow that with individual mime performances.

Suggested Mime Activities
Climbing a ladder
Walking in place
Hands on wall
The box
Throwing and catching a ball
Holding an object

Chapter 6
Verbal Individual Activities

Now you are ready to have your participants add speech to their established communication skills. Before you subject individuals to speaking in front of the whole group, I suggest you warm them up by having them express themselves in a one-on-one situation with which they are familiar. If necessary, go back and review "Circle Rotation"; its purpose then was to allow participants to meet one another. This time it will have a different purpose.

Getting Warmed Up

Circle Rotation Revisited

Objective: Students will be able to express various personal feelings and experiences to various members of the group.

Follow the same steps as before which will produce two circles of subjects facing one another in chairs. This time the exercise will be a lot more personal, but since the group has been working together for a while, this should not be too intimidating.

Round One: Tell us about a time ...

Announce to the group that the first round of topics will involve recalling and relating certain times in your life. Students will be given a statement to complete which will reveal personal feelings. Students should know that their stories can be real or made up.

Call out the first topic, allow time for each pair to relate responses to each other, and then call out "rotate" along with the next topic. It might help to designate the stationary group as starters to save time. Continue this pattern for one rotation and then stop.

Topic Examples
Tell us about a time you ...
... will never forget.
... wished for a miracle.
... were happiest for a member of your family.
... needed to talk to someone.
... felt just miserable.
... acted without thinking.

... wanted to escape.

... felt very needed.

... doubted your capabilities.

... remember hating someone or something.

... were sorry for something you'd done.

... liked someone the minute you met them.

... wished you could forget something or someone.

... were lonely.

... helped someone in need.

Round Two: Revelations

You can either continue in the same two circles or break into the two double circles as described in the original "Circle Rotation" activity. Students will be given a topic to consider before being asked to reveal a personal (or made up) experience.

Announce the first topic, allow time, call "rotate" with the next topic, etc.

Topics

An old enemy

Someone snobbish

How it would feel to meet a long-lost friend

A time when you were in a big hurry

How it feels to be your age

What it was like to be younger

A sad time when you cried

A time when you were very angry

What bores you the most

A time when you had to be extremely polite

A time when you felt shy or scared

A time when you were very cold (or warm)

A time when you were silly

A time when you felt out of control

A time when you tried to communicate with someone but failed

A time you had a problem with a machine

A trip you'd like to forget

Round Three: Express Yourself

Continue in the same circles or regroup if you wish. Clarify the focus of the next round and proceed as before.

Students will be given different situations and will be asked to consider how it would feel if given the situation happened to them.

After this series of experiences, the group should be sufficiently warmed up to proceed with speaking to the entire group. However, these first ventures need to be kept short so that they are less stressful.

Example Topics
How would it feel to find out that ...
... you were adopted?
... your parents are going to divorce?
... your family is moving out of state?
... your boy/girl friend is dating someone else?
... you're losing your hearing?
... you've won a million dollars?
... you are failing at school?
... all of your belongings have burnt up?
... you're pregnant (or about to become a father)?
... all of your money has been stolen?
... you are lost in a dangerous place?
... your mom and dad are really your grandparents?
... you've been fired and can't pay your bills?
... your house/apartment has been ransacked?
... you have a major assignment due in one week?

Monologues

Telephone Monologues
Objective: Students will be able to express themselves to the other members of the group as if they were carrying on a telephone conversation.

Since students are all comfortable with talking on the phone and little eye contact with the audience is required, this is a good place to start monologues. If you have a prop telephone to provide, place it on a small table next to a chair in the PA. This should be in the open end of a horseshoe circle. Using a sound to "ring in" promotes realism.

Have each participant draw his topic from your deck of cards, and proceed with the performances, going in order around the circle. While one performer is returning to his chair from the PA (to audience applause), the next will be making his way to the PA. There are three rounds of these monologues that will most likely cover several sessions. Be sure to clarify the variations in each round before distributing cards.

Be sure to instruct them to be realistic. For instance, it is important to allow appropriate wait time for the unheard portion of the conversation.

Round One: Outgoing Calls
Reasons to Call Someone

Accept an invitation

Make a friend

Get help when sick

Apply for a job

Reveal your anger

Gossip

Thank someone

Complain

Seek repairs

Express sympathy

Talk to a teacher

Report a crime

Bother someone you don't really know

Determine the cost of something

Ask for help

Help someone in trouble

Be funny

Apologize

Get information

Ask a favor

Relate bad news

Express happiness

Give out information

Hire someone

Order food

Sell something

Round Two: Incoming Calls
Who Calls and Why

Boss, to tell you you're fired

School counselor, to discuss unusual behavior

Police, to report the arrest of a relative

Baby brother, to complain about parents' punishment

Political candidate, to seek your vote

Clergyman, to ask about your weekly non-attendance

School administrator, to check on attendance

Doctor's office, to cancel an appointment

Bank, to report a bounced check

Salesperson, to sell magazines

Operator, to check on phone

Dentist's office, to indicate your checkup is due

Brother/sister, to say hello from college

Radio station, to announce a prize you've won

Wrong number

Your father, to ask about your homework

Former classmate, to tell you about a reunion

Fire department, to talk to you about smoke detectors

Fellow student, to get homework help
Teacher, to discuss your poor grades
Boy/girl, to discuss a date
Friend, to gossip
Mother, to let you know she's working late
Grandmother, to discuss her visit

Round Three: Reacting Appropriately

Example Emotions and Situations
Happiness — Someone invites you to a special place
Pride — Someone tells you you're promoted
Love — That special someone calls
Fear — A prank caller scares you
Sympathy — Someone tells you his troubles
Anger — Someone reveals a rumor
Sadness — Someone relates news of a death or injury
Hatred — An enemy calls to aggravate you
Excitement — You are given a chance to win a prize
Indecision — You have to agree on vacation plans with someone
Jealousy — Someone has something you want and calls to brag
Curiosity — Someone calls but won't reveal his identity
Surprise — Someone calls from whom you didn't expect to hear
Frustration — You are told that an appointment you need has been
              cancelled
Stress — Someone tells you about an upcoming test
Boredom — Someone to whom you didnt want to talk, calls
Distress — Someone calls with disturbing news
Exhaustion — Someone calls when you are sound asleep
Annoyance — A salesperson just won't give up
Dishonesty — The school calls for your parent and you pretend to
             be him/her

Think Out Loud

Objective: Students will be able to stand in front of the group and
deliver a monologue in which they think out loud about
an assigned topic.

For this series of monologues, use the horseshoe setup, but provide
no chair in the PA. Have participants draw cards from your deck and,
when called, walk to the PA, face the audience, and deliver the
monologue.

It is probably too soon yet to have these performances on a stage even if one is available. Use the same performance pattern you did in the last activity. Devote as many sessions as you wish to this.

The following groups of monologue topics call for participants to put themselves in the minds of various persons/objects/animals in a variety of situations.

Group #1
Elderly person waiting in line to cash a check
Artist trying to paint nude model for the first time
Policeman chasing speeders
Mother who is sick of her children
Shy teenager who wants a date
Homeless vagrant searching for food
Psychiatrist worried about his sanity
School principal needs to make a difficult announcement
Construction worker who likes to goof off
Five-year-old playing with dolls
Burglar who gets locked in the house he is robbing
Mature man/woman who wants to date boss
Husband/wife sick of deadbeat spouse
Bank president considering stealing money
Little dog who thinks he's ferocious
20-year-old lifeguard afraid of water
Wrestler about to get in the ring for the first time
Teacher who has to face a very difficult class

Group #2
Person considering suicide
Person in prison
A vampire about to bite
A being from outer space
Young child in bed in a dark room
Old person in a nursing home
A doll in a store
A caged animal
An insect

Group #3
Professional writer who can't think of an ending to his story
Oak tree about to be cut down for firewood
Airplane pilot who finds out he is going blind
Sales clerk who must make a sale or lose his job
College student who must pass exam to graduate
Ten-year-old who plays pranks and resents paybacks

Group #4

Very small child who is being led through a crowd of adults
Chicken about to be slaughtered
Baby in the womb about to be born
Chair which is about to be sat on by a heavy person
Pet who is anxiously waiting to be fed
Ant in someone's kitchen who sees the Raid can
Car which is tired of being abused by its owner
Infant who has been handled by one too many relatives
Wild animal that has been captured and sent to a zoo
Hungry fish that is tempted to bite the offered bait
Very small dog that sees a large dog approaching
Apple about to be picked from a tree and eaten
Shrub which is being approached by numerous dogs
Baby bird that tries to fly for the first time
Toy which has been purchased for a very nasty child

Group #5

An individual twin sensing the other's thoughts
Small child unable to walk
Person under hypnosis
Foreign visitor who speaks no English
Someone's conscience
A deaf mute
Someone's stomach revealing reactions to various foods
A person hospitalized and paralyzed
A person in a drug-altered state
Someone's guardian angel
Psychic who foresees disaster
Baby before birth
Gypsy fortune-teller

Group #6

Prisoner planning escape
Young girl who has to decide about abortion
Juror who has to decide about the death penalty
Person (non-speaking) who wants off life-support
Young man who receives draft notice
Student who has to face a strict dress code

Group #7

Infant who cannot communicate
Concerned parent of teenagers
Sole survivor of an accident
Person tempted to commit a crime
Child who has overheard that his parents are divorcing
Elderly person who wants to be young
Young person who has learned he is adopted

Group #8

Doctor discussing a small, unwilling child
Repairman in a filthy home
Girl/boy on first date
Athlete before game
Taxi driver after midnight
A drunk in a restaurant
A high-better at the race track
Bum in the park
Society person whose car breaks down in a rough neighborhood
Captain on his sinking ship
Psychiatrist getting treatment
Nun/priest at a modern movie
Streetwalker about annoying cop
Boater lost in the ocean
Off-duty principal about his job

Group #9

Criminal in jail
Babysitter discussing the job
Teen unhappy about hair/skin
Photographer about models
Celebrity discussing autograph hounds
Librarian discussing noisy kids
Secretary discussing an unfair boss
Psychiatrist discussing an unusual patient
Waiter discussing sore feet
Artist discussing lack of sales
Actor preparing for a role
Husband/wife discussing chores to be done
Hairdresser discussing a difficult customer
Teenager discussing parent's restrictions
Doctor with bad news to deliver

Teacher discussing papers to be marked
Salesperson discussing ugly merchandise
Young person who is lost
Clerk discussing long hours
Student discussing unfair grades
Fast-food server discussing a boring routine
Motorist discussing a traffic jam
Cop discussing fear for his life
Parent discussing kids in trouble
Lifeguard discussing bodies on the beach
Senior discussing the good-old-days
Kid discussing being so short

Group #10

Child afraid of the dark
Bag-person in the garbage
Stockbroker worried about the market
Supervisor planning to fire employee
Paper boy/girl delivering papers
Preacher tempted to steal
Determined athlete
Musician trying for a job
Beautician late for work
Housewife who wants a paying job

Group #11

Bird at feeder
Equipment in the playground
Boat with lost captain aboard
Desk in a classroom
Mirrors in a fun-house
Salt shaker in a restaurant
Clerk arranging products for display

Weed in the garden
Animal in danger
Ghost haunting a house
Martian arriving on Earth
Traffic light out of order
Food in the refrigerator

Place Topics

Objective: Students will be able to deliver a monologue to the group that expresses their reactions to being in a certain place. Students will practice using appropriate physical movements while speaking.

Here you begin to introduce physical movement into the monologue activity. At this point you might use a stage for performances or have the performers walk to the front of the audience who are seated in a straight line. Otherwise, follow the same procedure as before.

Topics

Express your reactions to being in the following places:

Underwater	In a time warp
In a submarine	On a sinking ship
In a burning building	In a cave
Lost in the wilderness	In an empty school
In a foreign country	In a hot-air balloon
In a convent	In a stalled elevator
In prison	In a cage
On a desert island	

You Are ...

Objective: Students will be able to deliver a monologue with appropriate physical movement as directed.

Follow the same procedures as in the previous activity.

Group #1

You are in a dangerous situation.
You are an unwed parent.
You are an adopted child.
You are a homeless person.
You are in an unusual situation.
You are an animal in the zoo.
You are the victim of a crime.
You are an abused appliance/vehicle.
You are a weed in a garden.
You are the keeper of a serious secret.
You are a hunted animal.
You are the husband/wife of an alcoholic.

You are a lost puppy.
You are walking down the aisle at your wedding.
You are the coach of a losing team.
You are a teacher on vacation.
You are a piece of furniture on sale.
You are an item about to be dumped.

Group #2
You are a soldier stranded in a mine field.
You can't shake the feeling that someone is trying to kill you.
You are alone in the house at the mercy of your older brother/sister.
You are trapped in a cave that you were exploring.
You are unable to move your legs as a result of an accident.
You return to your car to find the keys locked inside.
You are a robber who gets locked in a closet during an attempted robbery.
You are helpless in a wheelchair and the electricity goes out.
You are locked in a vault during a bank robbery.

Group #3
You wake up with no memory.
You are in jail for a crime you didn't commit.
You are a textbook in the hands of a high school student.
You are a 25-year-old piece of furniture in its original home.
You are a TV set about to be traded in.
You are an animal about to be slaughtered for food.
You are pregnant and about to deliver alone.
You are the devil about to face God.
You are desperate for money.
You are the walls of a room overhearing dangerous secrets.
You are responsible for an accident.
You have suddenly shrunk in size.
You're awaiting important diagnostic results.
The vacation of your dreams becomes a nightmare.
You believe that a dream you had is a warning.
You overhear a terrible rumor about your best friend.
You are a sick dog in a small pet shop cage.
You have pre-marriage doubts.
You are on a serious diet and in a candy store.
You feel guilty about someone's handicap.
Your brother/sister makes fun of you.
You flunk out of school.
You are the only witness to a crime.

Problems, Problems, Problems!

Objective: Students will be able to deliver a monologue with appropriate physical movements that express their feelings about a problematic situation.

Students will express their feelings about problematic situations. Use the same procedure as previously and incorporate as many of the following topics as you wish.

Topics

You suspect your son/daughter is into drugs.

You are not getting along with your parents.

You are thinking about suicide.

You weigh 80 pounds but think you're fat.

You have symptoms of a disease but are afraid to tell.

You're overweight but can't stick to a diet.

A friend is getting hooked on gambling.

You suspect your husband/wife is unfaithful.

You married young and now want a divorce.

You just moved to town and can't make friends.

You dropped out of school and now regret it.

You've been told you have an incurable disease and don't know how to cope.

You've discovered an attraction to the opposite sex and are concerned.

You like a popular girl/guy but are too shy to approach.

You've told your best friend an embarrassing secret and find out it's been spread around the whole school.

You are serious about being attracted to a much older person.

You're worried about your parent's drinking problem.

You can't overcome your addiction to cigarettes.

You lost all your money at a casino and can't pay your bills.

Speeches

This series calls for participants to express factual opinions rather than feelings and emotions. Point out that each speaker must express an opinion even if it is made up or the speaker is unsure about it. If these are young people, they may not yet have opinions on many of these topics.

Controversial Topics

Objective: Students will be able to stand in front of the group to express their opinions on controversial topics, giving at least three supporting reasons/examples and a summary statement.

Plan time is required here. After distributing topics (selected from cards), give each person a plan sheet (details to follow), and have them spread out around the meeting area. During planning time, you should circulate to answer questions and give suggestions as needed. When ready, have everyone return to the original area and have the speeches presented.

The plan sheet should include areas for the performer to plan the following elements: Speaker, topic, introduction, attention-getting device, intentions stated, at least three supporting reasons, examples to support view, summary.

Controversial Topics

War	Welfare
Unwed parenting	Women's rights
Civil liberties	Juvenile delinquency
Sex education	Mandatory AIDS testing
Right to die	Animal rights
The homeless	Drug abuse
Extended school year	Teen drinking
Child abuse	Gun control
Divorce	The speed limit
Arranged marriages	Gambling
Capital punishment	Legalized drugs
Interracial marriage	Foreign aid
Drunk driving	The drinking age
Abortion	School uniforms
Cults	

One-Minute Speeches

Objective: Students will be able to deliver a one-minute speech to the group in an assigned format.

Planning time is again required. Since it is not necessary that each participant have a different speech format, prepare enough cards for all participants, repeating formats as necessary.

Distribute the cards, allow planning time (you circulate), and have the students present their speeches. Have a timing device that sounds at the end of one minute to signal the speech is ended. If no such device is available, use a stopwatch and call time yourself. Do not allow the speaker to stop speaking before the signal is given or continue speaking after the minute is up.

Suggested Formats

Election/appointment (for self or someone else)
Sales pitch
Opinion
Entertainment
Serious happening (real/imaginary)
Editorial (local/other)
Hobby
Biography (self/other)
Review (book/music/TV/movie)

Nonsense Speeches

Objective: Students will be able to communicate a topic to the members of the group using only nonsense words and physical movements.

This activity should provide a little comic relief from the more traditional speeches you have been doing. After reviewing the directions, you can either provide topics or let students come up with their own.

Students are told that they must try to express themselves using only one sound ("Blah," "Na," etc.), which can be repeated as needed/desired. After a brief planning period, have the students present their speeches.

After each speech, the audience will guess the topic. The correctness of the guesses following each speech should be acknowledged by the speaker. If the guessing goes on too long, ask the speaker to reveal the topic.

Note: Emphasize the importance of speed, volume, facial expressions, hand gestures, body movements, etc.

Miscellaneous Activities

Oral Reading/Interpretation

Objective: Students will be able to read a short written selection to the group in an appropriately dramatic manner.

Each student will be assigned or choose an appropriate, short written selection. This may be a short story or a portion of a longer one.

Planning time should be provided, during which students may form pairs and practice reading aloud.

Students will present their oral selections to the group. An evaluation procedure may be used if desired.

Note: Students should be asked to refrain from reading from their selection without looking up.

Intonation/Meaning

Objective: Students will be able to express to the group different feelings using simple words.

Prepare two decks of cards, one with suggested words and the other with feelings. Distribute one card of each type to every participant. After a brief planning time, proceed with the resulting presentations. If time permits, repeat the activity so that participants have a chance to work with multiple feelings and words.

Suggestions

Words: Hello, what?, no, yes, oh, etc.
Feelings: Flirtatious, surprised, disappointed, to get attention, etc.

Personality Interviews

Objective: Students will be able to assume the role of a famous person and be interviewed by members of the group in order to determine their identities.

Each participant is designated as a particular well-known person. He stands in front of the group and answers questions directed to him by members of the audience. The audience's goal is to find out who the performer is impersonating.

To ensure that the entire audience is involved, establish a pattern for questions such as starting on the far right side of the group and working your way left. On an audience member's turn, she can either ask a question or guess the speaker's identity. The performance concludes when the correct identity is determined or the leader calls "time" and the speaker reveals his identity.

Notes: Responses to questions must be as honest as possible, but "I'm not sure" is an acceptable response if necessary.

There will, of course, be forbidden questions such as "Who are you?" Off-limits questions should be established before beginning the activity.

Hat Grab Bag

Objective: Students will be able to present character monologues based on the particular hats they receive.

The instructor should gather a large bag of various hats (thrift stores or garage sales can be good, affordable sources). Students will select a hat at random from the bag and plan a short scene that incorporates the hat.

Notes: The hat does not have to be worn during the scene, but must play a significant role. You may choose to allow the use of other performers in the scenes, but credit for the activity should still be given to the individual.

This activity can be done with articles of clothing or objects as well.

Video Clips

Objective: Students will be able to prepare and present to the group a portion of film representing a specific area of quality.

Students are given the following assignment with time to prepare outside of class and assigned date(s) of presentation.

Assignment

Select a short (no more than five minutes) portion of a film which features an excellent representation of one of the following categories: drama, humor, animation, suspense, special effects, music. Prepare a verbal introduction for the clip which includes the following:

1. Name of selection
2. Category of excellence
3. Your reason for selecting the clip
4. Any other appropriate information (actors' names, background info, etc.) you feel is useful.

When you present, you will introduce the clip, show the clip, and then give a brief summary, including time to take questions from the audience.

Note: It is extremely important to insist that the clips be set at the correct starting spot. This will avoid wasted time which will interfere with the flow of the activity. Obviously the amount of time for each clip can be adjusted to suit the number or participants/time available for the activity. It is also wise to set standards which are appropriate to the participants. This can be done using movie ratings or some other designated method.

Chapter 7
Verbal Pair Activities

Now that your group members have practiced their nonverbal skills and experienced speaking individually, they should be ready for pair activities, particularly improvisation.

Improvised Scenes

First Liners

Objective: Working in pairs, students will be able to improvise short scenes that begin with a specific line.

This activity was without a doubt the most popular and versatile of them all. It begins as a basic pair activity, but there are variations that allow it to expand into a far more complex group activity. For now, we will use it to begin the verbal pair activities.

Begin with the group in a large circle. Have the opening lines on cards ready to be drawn as each pair is formed. Send the person to your right into the middle of the circle, and have the person to your left draw a card. He should read it silently, return it to you, and join his partner in the middle of the circle.

The performer who drew the card says the line, and the conversation begins. The improvisation must continue until you say "Curtain!" Do not let these run on too long, especially at the beginning. Many of these will develop into arguments, but that shouldn't be a problem.

Examples of First Lines:

Group #1:

I hate you!	I never want to see you again.
Good-bye.	I'll always love you.
I hope you die.	I'll miss you.
Don't forget what you promised.	Catch ya later!
Take care of yourself.	And you'd better be there.
I'll get even, you wait.	Call you later.
Please don't tell anyone.	Why should I trust you?
Write me soon.	And behave yourself.
You're crazy.	

Group #2:

Why is your nose bleeding?
I want to know how you got this job.
I can stand on my head for an hour!
Your little sister imitates everything you do.
Why can't you get along with your parents?
Where is my money?
Now just do exactly what I do.
I love flying, don't you?
Can I carry those for you?
Will you please help me across the street?
I told you before — clean the area, now!
Psst, your zipper's open!
How can I forget the terrible things you've said?
Well, how do you like your new hairdo?
This picture proves what you've been up to.
But honestly, purple is your color.
Please read the directions before you ask questions.
Is it possible for you to be quiet?
Your dress is magnificent.
Don't you just love this song?
Now put your right foot there and your left foot here.
Take off your shoes immediately!
Why do you have that silly smile on your face?
Here, pour this in there and drink it down.
Why is your face so red?
I love turnips, don't you?
Lean back, and just enjoy.

Group #3:

Why me?
Can you sing?
Don't I know you from somewhere?
Do you have change for a fifty?
Now, what would you like to order?
But I told you, you're a dollar short.
Is your name really Abraham?
I saw the best movie yesterday.
Your sister is really pretty.
Wait 'til I get you home!
How much is it worth to you?
Play my favorite song.
You're OK when you want to be.

Listen to your mother.
Wait for me!
I love your new outfit.
Let me by, please!
What time is it?
Move quickly!
Better not eat that!
Can't you be nice?
Did you tell Susie?
Sorry I'm late.
Do you mind?
Roll over and die!

Group #4:

I want my mommy!
Did you see that gorgeous guy?
Feel how soft the fur is.
Do you expect me to believe that?
What is that you're wearing?
Hamster brain!
Police, police!
Have a light?
Read them their rights.
I said a size six.
Just take a little off the top.
You're so cute when you're angry.
You've been nothing but trouble since you were born.

Now, tell me all about it.
Who did that?
Right or wrong?
Wait a minute!
You're adopted!
Get your paws off me!
Shut up!
Please hug me!
I won, I won!
You look great in that color.
That's way too much money.
Can I borrow it, please?

Group #5:

Oh, you are such a fool.
Can I have some?
Don't you dare!
Where did you get that hat?
Please try to be there, please.
Will you pray for me?
Just who do you think you are?
One day you'll miss me.
Is this your wallet?
Did you clean your room?
Are you sure you can afford it?
No wonder your mother worries about you.

Follow me, now!
Am I lucky?
What is your problem?
Aren't you a little old for that?
I told you before, didn't I?
Behave yourself.
Oh come on, ask him out!
Oh, what a cute puppy.
Happy Halloween!
Is it your birthday?
You walk ahead, OK?

Seasonal

Prepare a list of First-liners to start pair conversations according to the regular procedure; however, make them seasonal to suit the occasion.

For example, the following could be used prior to/around Thanksgiving:

Gobble, gobble, gobble!
Make a wish!
Ten dollars says my team wins!
Come and get it!
And what grade are you in now?
Touchdown!
OK, everybody in the car!

Hey! I wanted the drumstick!
Man, am I stuffed!
Hi, Grandma!
My, how you've grown!
Pass the gravy, please!
Aw, you brought the baby!
See ya next year!

Excuse me.
Move over and let me in.
Will you carve?
Go, team, go!
Now, let's get everyone together for a picture.
Why, it's been ages since I've seen you.
Happy holidays, everyone!

Coffee, anyone?
Seconds, anyone?
Please pass your plate.
So — what's new?

End Liners

Objective: Working in pairs, students will be able to improvise short scenes based on a line that they must use to end the scene.

This activity is similar to "First Liners," except that each pair of participants is given the line to *end* their scene. This time both participants will know the line, and some planning time must be provided. Each pair should strive to use the line to realistically close the scene.

Suggested End Liners:

You just wait!
You'd better be right!
Absolutely not!
I forgive you.
Your luck just ran out!
I quit!
Not guilty!

Now, get lost!
I told you so.
OK, I give up!
I never want to see you again!
I'll never forget you.
I still care.
Have a nice day!

Scene Starters

Objective: Working in pairs, students will be able to improvise short scenes based on phrases or sentences assigned.

Use the horseshoe set up or a straight line in front of the stage. Distribute cards with various scene-starters to random pairs. After planning time is provided, the resulting scenes should be presented.

Suggested Scene Starters

Group #1:
The little man grinned at Jerry.
He picked up the rifle.
A chubby girl in pigtails sat down near me.

51

Claire sat on the end of the bench.
Marilyn glanced nervously at the man.
Shelly set the package on the table.
The door of Henry's room opened slowly.
Joey giggled.
He touched the girl's hair.
The child said, "I'm scared."
The girl's mother was dead.
Daddy came home late at night.
Promptly at six, the doorbell rang.
Molly turned fifteen.
The old man woke to find a moonlit room.
I nervously pushed open the door.
The air was heavy and full of haze.
Next, the women said …
Gig belched softly.
Carrie was a tall, thin girl.
Herman had big brown eyes and fuzzy hair.
The snow fell softly as I walked home.
I hate it when you act like a child.

Group #2:

Now sit down and relax.
I demand perfection.
Hold it right there.
I don't want to scare you but …

Unusual:

Why are you swallowing a goldfish?
Why are you secretly letting a horse out of a fenced pasture?
Why are you tearing up a letter?
Why are you throwing out a steak you just cooked?
Why are you burning the homework you just finished?
Why are you putting a gun in a drawer?
Why are you selling a diamond ring you promised you'd always
    keep?
Why are you sneaking into the gorilla cage at the zoo?
Why are you making a quick trip to a flower shop?

Two-line:
a. What a beautiful day; do you mind if I open the windows?
b. No, go ahead.

a. You've got to be kidding; did I really win?
b. Yes, you are now $10,000 richer!

a. Don't bother to explain; I don't want to hear it.
b. But Mom, I have a good excuse.

a. I feel sick; did you put something in my food?
b. Are you crazy? Why would I do that?

a. But officer, I only had one beer!
b. Really? You seem pretty unsteady to me.

a. But I'm sure I left my pocketbook right here.
b. Sorry, I didn't see it.

a. How can I prove to you that I'm telling the truth?
b. I don't think after all the lies that it's possible.

a. How can I concentrate when you're singing?
b. Sorry, I wasn't thinking; forgive me?

a. Watch out! The teacher's looking this way.
b. Gee, thanks; all I need is more trouble.

a. Why are you always late?
b. I'm not always late; I'm just late today.

a. Did you see that creepy looking guy?
b. Yeah, what do you think he's up to?

a. Move out of my way; I've got to get in there!
b. But you might get killed.

a. But I told you, I'm not going to school.
b. As long as you're living under my roof, you'll do as I say!

Questions:
Note: Avoid using yes or no questions.
Why don't you mind your own business?
What are you doing in my room?
Why didn't you wait for me?
Alright, what's the big secret?
Who do you think you are?
What do you think is going to happen?
What do you dream about the most?

Advertisements

Reality

Objective: Working in pairs, students will be able to present an advertisement that promotes a real product with an original name.

For this activity and the next, follow similar set-up and topic-assignment procedures to those used in "Scene Starters."

Assign each pair of participants a product area (see below). They should decide what specific product they will advertise from that area. While it must be a real product, it should not be one which is already named. For example, it can be a soda, but not Pepsi.

All ads should include: An original name for the product, a price or price range, and product appeal (what makes people want to purchase it?). Both members of the team should be involved in the planning of the ad, and both must participate in its presentation. Use of visual aides is optional.

Product Areas

Vehicle	Beverage
Toy	Food
Health (other than weight)	Hair care
Clothing	Weight
Skin care	Appliance
Cosmetic	Dental
Sports	Electronic
Paper	Cleaning

Fantasy

Objective: Working in pairs, students will be able to present to the group an advertisement promoting an imaginary product.

Assign each pair a product area (Use the same list of product areas in "Reality"). The pair must identify a specific product from that area which does not already exist (the product does something which cannot be done in reality). The ad requirements are the same as in "Reality."

Examples

A cream that grows hair on bald heads
A pill that makes one stronger
A memory pill
A self-correcting pen
A complete-meal capsule
A thinning cream
A coordinated-outfit-selection machine
An instant-tan spray
An instant weight-loss formula
A disguise for sleeping through class or work
A phone which puts potential customers in a good mood
A machine that does homework or housework

The following lists may come in handy for students needing a bit more inspiration.

Types of Ads

A famous person endorsing a product
Anti-drug ad
Cash-rebate with purchase
Testimonials from people who have used the product
    (before and after)
Teen-oriented
Clever song/jingle
Comparison/survey
Vacation-of-a-lifetime offer
Taste test

Types of Products

Anti-wrinkle	Stain-removal
Computer dating service	New-style vehicle
Pain release	Stop smoking clinic
Wardrobe planning	Beauty makeover
Housework helper	Stress release

Other Topic Areas

Cultural product	Electronic product
Musical product	Old-age product

Scenes of Conflict/Problems

Go over the essentials (see below) for scenes involving conflict. If available, use a short video to illustrate this material. (The old silent film of Laurel and Hardy selling Christmas trees in California is perfect. This can be found in Robert Youngson's *When Comedy Was King* featuring Laurel and Hardy in *Big Business*.) Showing students a basic plot diagram (rising action, climax, falling action, etc.) would also be helpful.

The Essentials

Any scene involving conflict has certain basic elements. The scene starts with a static situation where nothing much is happening. A character called the protagonist arrives on the scene and has a goal to achieve. He runs into problems because of a person or force who provides opposition to his goals. This person or force is called the antagonist. The rest of the scene features increasingly intense conflicts between these two persons/forces until one wins out. This point is called the climax; after the climax, the action subsides.

Examples: A customer and bartender argue over serving another drink; a salesperson and customer argue over buying a product.

Knock, Knock!

Objective: Working in pairs, students will be able to improvise a short scene that illustrates the elements of conflict.

Assign a character and a related goal to one member of the pair. The scene starts when this person knocks on the door of the other to achieve his goal. The scene continues until the goal is reached or the person gives up.

Possible characters: salesperson, girl/boy friend, relative, etc.
Possible goals: to sell, to apologize, to borrow something, etc.

Example Conflicts
Group #1:
Person wants relative to get a job
Beggar wants money from a pedestrian
Kid wants to move in with a relative
Kid wants parent to let him have a party
Person wants a relative to quit smoking
Kid wants to marry someone his parents dislike
Kid wants to run away from home
Kid wants money from his parent
Kid wants to quit school
Person wants a relative to quit drinking

Group #2:
Doctor and patient argue over diagnosis
Brother and sister argue over shared room
Teacher and student argue over grades
Roommates argue over money
Boss and employee argue over working conditions
Policeman and suspect argue over arrest
Parent and child argue over bedtime
Beautician and customer argue over hairdo
Girl and boy argue over relationship

Problems/Challenges

Objective: Working in pairs, students will be able to improvise a short scene concerning problems to overcome and/or challenges to face.

Problems:
The following situations can be assigned to pairs of participants. Each involves a problem encountered which needs to be overcome. Planning time should be provided before presentation.

Situations:
Repairman is called to a filthy home and greeted by the owner.
Boater is lost in the ocean and has a conversation with an angel.
Streetwalker/runaway is approached by a cop and has to answer his questions.

Off-duty principal talks to a friend about his job.
Religious person attends a current movie, and his reactions affect the other attendees.
Ship's captain must deal with a difficult passenger.
Pediatrician must deal with an unwilling patient.
Person bets the last of his money at the racetrack.
Taxi driver has a difficult early-morning passenger.
Bum approaches a stranger in the park for money.
Wealthy person is forced to ask directions from a low-class person.
Rookie athlete in locker room before the game gets no help from the veterans.
Psychiatrist needs to seek help for his own problems.
Drunken customer causes difficulty for waitress in restaurant.

Challenges:

Same directions as above; these situations involve challenges which people have to face.

Situations:

Elderly person is learning to drive.
Owner is trying to supervise the construction of his own house.
Person is trying to follow difficult directions for putting a child's toy together.
Man is trying to sew his clothing.

Scenes Based on Places

Places

Objective: Working in pairs, students will be able to improvise short scenes focusing on specific places.

The following scene suggestions will be assigned to pairs of participants. Each involves a specific place as a central focus. Planning time should be provided prior to presentation.

You Are There!

Situation	Place
The machines do not operate properly.	Laundromat
The flight has been delayed.	Airport
Teaching little brother or sister to cook	Kitchen
Librarian is making too much noise.	Library
Your child is misbehaving.	Grocery store
Trying to decide on a purchase	Department store

58

Places, places!

Broadway chorus line	Hot air balloon
Art gallery	In an egg
In a TV set	In a shoe
Church	In a lightbulb
Jail cell	Inside a clock
A shower	Rowboat
Fish bowl	In a trash can
Inside a toothpaste tube	Beehive
Wind tunnel	Space capsule
Operating room	Restaurant
In a mother's womb	Store window
In a straightjacket	Barbershop
Swimming pool	Car
Playpen	Maze

Scenes Based on Character

Character Scenes

Objective: Working in pairs, students will be able to improvise short scenes based on a variety of characters and situations. (The following series of scene suggestions will all fall under the same basic objective.)

The following situations can be assigned to pairs of participants. Each is based on a type of person/character. Planning time should be provided before presentations.

Character/Actions

Mix and match the following characters and actions and assign to pairs of participants. Different combinations should produce a variety of resulting scenes. Planning time should be provided before presentation.

Characters:

Students	Policemen
Children	Actors
Prisoners	Housewives/husbands

Actions:

Hiding	Escaping
Selling	Gambling
Sleeping	Hunting
Flying a kite	Washing windows
Washing a car	Giving away money
Stacking wood	Typing a letter
Raking a lawn	Calling long distance
Bridling a horse	Ironing clothes
Watching a sunset	Shoveling snow
Singing a song	Shaking rugs
Digging a ditch	Cutting a lawn
Picking flowers	Dissecting a frog
Changing a tire	Chopping wood
Robbing a bank	

Character/Line

Provide different lists, which can be on cards to be drawn. Pair members select one card from each list and use plan time provided to create a short scene coordinating the items.

Characters:

Diners at restaurant counter	Children
Employees	Patients in doctor's office
Brothers/sisters	Old folks
Students	High school dropouts
Commuters	Boy/Girl Scouts
Drivers at traffic light	Police officers
Homeless people	Teachers

Lines:

Wait a minute, I was here first!
I bet you can't run as fast as me.
How come you got a raise and I didn't?
What's wrong with you?
I won't tell if you don't.
Remember the good old days?
Where do you get off looking over here?
So, why did you quit?
Boy, have I had a day!
I think we're really lost this time.
Hey, what do you think you're doing?

Say, why don't we get that guy?
Can you spare a dollar?
What is wrong with kids nowadays?

Character/Ages

Assign the various types of people/ages to pairs of participants. Allow plan time before presentation.

Characters and Ages:

Burglar, 38

Sculptor, 44

Unemployed dropout, 18

Bank executive, 40

Homemaker, 33

Used car dealer, 50

Librarian, 63

Model, 22

Store clerk, 22

Prison guard, 55

Social worker, 30

Waiter/waitress, 28

Retired letter carrier, 70

Paper boy/girl, 13

Clergy, 45

College student, 20

Teacher, 51

Character/Clue Words

Mix and match the following characters and clue words and assign to pairs of participants. Plan time should be provided to prepare appropriate scenes that incorporate the characters and clue words.

Group #1:

Characters:

Drug addict

Custodian

High-pressure salesman

Vending machine repair person

Off-duty police officer

High-fashion model

Teenage runaway

Homeless vagrant

Person in need of organ transplant

First-year college student

Conceited movie star

Very timid housewife/husband

Secretary to an executive

Department store Santa

Member of religious order

Concerned veterinarian

Famous political figure

Poor, recently-adopted child

Clue words:

Date	Sorry	Divorce
Parents	Accident	Innocent
Ugly	Rehearsal	Confrontation
Different	Flight	

Group #2:

Characters (in pairs):

Drug pusher, undercover cop	Surfer, lifeguard
Talking mailbox, small child	Janitor, teenager
Police officer, shopper	Bartender, 18-year-old
Landscaper, talking animal	Airline steward, passenger
Bus driver, little-old-lady/man	Vacationer, host/hostess
TV personality, fan	Ticket collector, patron

Clue words:

Magazine	Underwear	Coins
Invisible	Pneumonia	Machete
Gold		

Relationships

Assign the following situations to pairs to plan and present appropriate scenes.

Group #1:

Roommates — One thinks it's too expensive to go out for the evening, and the other is tired of staying home.

Classmates — One is put in charge of the other while the teacher leaves the room.

Siblings — One forces the other to clean the room.

Parent/child — Parent demands to know where child is going.

Siblings — One has borrowed from the other without asking.

Tourist/guide — Tourist is not happy with the guide's program.

Teacher/student — Student doesn't want to admit that material is too difficult.

Salesperson/customer — Salesperson is frustrated when customer can't decide on purchase.

Parent/child — Child must reveal that he wrecked the car.

Friends — One has hit the other for seemingly no reason.

Roommates — Roommates disagree on selection of new apartment.

Robber/victim — Victim protests he has no money when robber demands it.

Friends — One is threatening to commit suicide.

Taxi driver/passenger — Passenger is confused about where he wants to be driven.

Siblings — One is packing to run away.

Group #2:

Friends pack car for a trip.
Roommates discuss decorations.
Cheerleaders plan a routine.
Students decorate for a dance.
Parent/child discuss curfew.
Family members go on a camping trip.
Parent/child discuss future plans.
Friends discuss money owed.
Friends discuss relationship problems.
Siblings argue over chores.

People/Places

Assign the following people and places to pairs to plan and present appropriate scenes.

Pair	Place
Barber, customer	Barber shop
Lawyer, client	Jail
Psychiatrist, patient	Office
Parent, child	Home
Drug addict, counselor	Hospital
Person, computer	Computer room
King or queen, servant	Castle
Scientist, monster	Laboratory
Waiter, customer	Restaurant
Clergyman, alcoholic	Church
Beggar, business person	Street
Coach, player	Locker room

Conversations

Assign the following conversation situations to pairs to plan and present appropriate scenes.

Group #1:

Patients share their worries in the waiting room.
Employees relax in lounge during break.
Couple parting after first date.
Roommates share confidences.
Celebrity speaks to journalist.
Prospective in-law chats with parent.
Relatives reunited after separation.
Client discussing apartment rental with owner.

Grandparent lecturing grandchild.
Friends discuss parents' divorces.
Big brother/sister gives younger sibling advice.
Counselor counsels troubled person.
Parent explains the facts to a child.
Doctor has bad news for the patient.

Group #2:
(The pair-conversations below will all concern money.)

Boss, employee	Director, auditioner
Doctor, patient	Salesperson, customer
Roommate, roommate	School personnel, student
Parent, child	Waiter, customer
Friend, friend	Counselor, client
Lawyer, client	Judge, accused
Police officer, suspect	

Special Scenes

Personal Quality
Objective: Working in pairs, students will be able to improvise a scene reflecting the personal quality assigned.

Students are assigned a personal quality and present a scene that reflects the assigned quality. The audience may guess the quality.

Qualities

Vanity	Superiority	Revenge
Snobbery	Nervousness	Emotionalism
Anxiety		

Traumatic
Objective: Working in pairs, students will be able to improvise a scene reflecting a traumatic experience.

Students are assigned a traumatic experience and present a scene that reflects the assigned experience.

Traumatic Experiences

A young person about to be married is told he has an incurable disease.

A person who is proud of his family background finds out that his father is a criminal.

A brilliant scientist finds out that he is going blind.

A defector is told that the family he left behind has been tortured since his escape.

A parent learns that his only child has been kidnapped.

Opposites

Objective: Working in pairs, students will be able to improvise a scene reflecting opposite situations.

Students are assigned an opposite situation and present a scene that reflects the assigned situation.

Opposite Situations

A shy person must work with an outgoing person on a project.

A less attractive person befriends an attractive person hoping to gain acceptance.

A stylishly dressed person attempts to teach an unstylishly dressed person the art of dressing.

An older person has to share his vacation with a much younger person with different tastes than his own.

A sloppy/lazy person moves in with a tidy/energetic person hoping that work will get done.

An executive person is forced to hire and train someone with little skill and less drive.

An athletic person attempts to coach a less-skilled person in his special sport.

A scared/nervous person is trapped in a stalled elevator with a brave/proud person.

A childless person is forced into conversation with someone who has many offspring.

Change/Contrast

Objective: Working in pairs, students will be able to improvise a scene reflecting a dramatic change.

Students are assigned a dramatic change and present a scene that reflects the assigned change.

Dramatic Changes

Speediness to slowness
Confidence to fear
Youth to old age
Aggressiveness to timidity

Anger to acceptance
Pity to envy
Neatness to carelessness
Honesty to dishonesty

Seasonal Contrast

Objective: Working in pairs, students will be able to improvise a scene reflecting seasonal contrast.

During the Christmas/New Year's season, students are assigned a seasonal contrast and present a scene that reflects the assigned contrast.

Seasonal Contrasts

Excited to open present, disappointed with result
Frustrated to find the right gift, happy when found
Scared that Santa will not come, happy when he does
Grumpy about the holiday fuss, pleased when included
Angry about having no plans for New Year's Eve, happy when plans are made
Tired of waiting on gift-seekers, happy to help small child
Sad when alone for the holiday, happy when joined by peers
Unhappy when short of money for gifts, happy when able to earn more
Excited that friend will be home for the holiday, unhappy to hear about friend's change of plans
Happy to be invited to a party, disappointed when left alone there
Excited to go see Santa, frightened when on Santa's lap
Unhappy that relative will not be home, surprised when he shows up
Frustrated when unable to find the perfect tree, pleased when you do

Helpful

Objective: Working in pairs, students will be able to improvise a scene reflecting someone helping another.

Students are assigned a situation in which someone helps another and present a scene that reflects the assigned situation.

Helpful Situations

A person who thinks everyone forgot his birthday is cheered by a special gift.

A younger person goes to someone older to discuss his problem.

An employee who has heard how tough the boss is finds out otherwise.

A homeless person is surprised to find out that someone cares and is trying to help.

An experienced worker takes pity on an inexperienced one and tries to help him adjust.

A child who gets separated from his parent in a large store gets help from an unexpected source.

A new student arrives in school and is unexpectedly befriended by someone.

A child who has been scared by a fierce storm is comforted by a previously hateful babysitter.

Fantasy

Objective: Working in pairs, students will be able to improvise a scene reflecting a fantasy situation.

Students are assigned a fantasy situation and present a scene that reflects the assigned situation.

Fantasy Situations

Clothes in a store talk about how stupid the people look who are trying them on.

Bottles of alcohol in a liquor store talk about what they'd like to do to the people who purchase them.

Animals in a pet shop talk about how they've been mistreated.

Appliances in the kitchen talk about the abuse they take.

Fruits and vegetables in a market tell how it feels to be squeezed and manhandled by the customers.

Cosmetics on a dresser talk about the looks of the people who use them.

Newborn babies comment to each other about the people who stare at them through the nursery window.

Focus on You!

Objective: Students will be able to involve themselves in a logical manner in improvisations begun by their partners; or, they will be able to begin improvisations in which their partners will become involved.

Provide one of the pair members with a situation. That member begins a scene based on the situation assigned. The other member of the pair must involve himself in a logical manner.

Situations

A hypnotist helps you overcome problems.

A teacher provides you with someone to talk to.

You join a commune to escape life.

Your boss tries to guide you for your own good.

A family member provides needed support.

A friendly stranger is a sounding board.

Religion gives you the answer you've been seeking.

A psychiatrist tries to help you.

You go to the police to confess.

Your husband/wife tries to help you face your troubles.

You become frustrated when nothing you do to your hair seems to help.

You become angry when you are turned down for a job you think you deserve.

You get excited when you think you have won lots of money.

You become dependent on a boy/girl friend who has helped you with some problems.

You become curious when an unusually shaped package arrives at your house.

You become frantic when you think someone is breaking into your house.

You are confused about how to find your way out of a crowded situation.

You get nervous when asked to speak in front of a large group of people.

You become depressed when you hear that a close friend is seriously ill.

You become demanding when an employee of yours fails to follow directions.

You become careful when you find yourself in a dangerous situation.

You become proud when you find out that you are going to be a father/mother.

Miscellaneous

It's All in How You Say It!

Objective: Students will be able to initiate or involve themselves in improvisations starting with a common word that is expressed in a specific way.

Common words spoken in different ways are used to start two-person scenes. You may assign words to pairs or let them choose their own.

Examples

Common Words:

Yes   Oh   What   Hello

Ways to Express Common Words:

Emphatically   Cautiously
As if answering the phone   As if in pain
Sarcastically   In anger
As a question   Demandingly
Dramatically   Humorously
Suspiciously   As if disappointed
In surprise   Flirtatiously
To get attention
As if to someone who is hard of hearing

Interview for Opinion

Objective: Students will be able to improvise a scene in which they either interview or are interviewed by a partner.

One of the pair participants interviews the other in one of the following situations.

Situations

Salesperson interviews shopper about his eating habits.
Survey-taker interviews person about political views.
Photographer interviews model about posing.
News reporter interviews celebrity for live TV.
Psychiatrist interviews patient about sanity.
Employer interviews person about unusual job.
School principal interviews teacher for a job.
Talk-show host interviews entertainer about personal life.

Clothing Scenes

Objective: Working in pairs, students will be able to improvise a scene based on items of clothing.

List various items of clothing and assign one to each pair. Scenes should be developed around the assigned items.

Possible Items of Clothing

Sandals and shorts
Gym shorts
Insulated underwear
Torn apron
Felt hat with feather
Dirty coveralls

White shirt and sport jacket
Cowboy hat and boots
Bow tie and cummerbund
Paint-splattered T-shirt
Tight leather pants

Sensory

Objective: Working in pairs, students will be able to improvise two scenes, one that features the sense they are assigned, and the other that features the loss of that sense.

Assign each pair one of the senses. Each pair should prepare two scenes — one featuring the use of that sense, and the other the loss of that sense.

Note: Depending on how many people are in the group, there may be more than one pair per sense.

Senses

Smell	Hearing	Taste
Touch	Sight	ESP

No Laughing Matter

Objective: Students will be able to participate in a series of pair improvisations in which the goal is to make their partners laugh.

Use a circle set up for this series of short scenes, with the PA in the middle.

Select one pair of participants to start. Assign one of them the task of trying to make the other laugh (this can be done only verbally, not physically). When someone laughs, he is replaced by another participant and the activity continues. (It's easiest to replace participants in sequence around the circle.) If, after a designated period of time, there is no laughter, the provoker is replaced by another participant and the activity continues.

Recitation/Evaluation

Objective: Working in pairs, students will be able to perform the scene from a written play as directed.

Pairs of students should be given (or told to select) a portion of a play (appropriate length and content to be determined by the leader). Keep the selections short and understandable, especially if you require students to memorize the scene. Once scenes are selected, the following procedure should be applied:

- Students in each pair should copy the selection.
- Students should decide on the roles (if there are more than two roles, they might double).
- Students are given time to practice.
- Recitations are presented and evaluated (if desired).

Note: More time can be designated for memorization of the script, and presentation can be done with the assistance of a prompter.

Optional Evaluation

Observing classmates can make value judgments using the following categories:

Were lines delivered smoothly?

Were there meaningful pauses?

Was the passage appropriate?

Did the students deliver lines at an appropriate speed/rate?

Was there clear enunciation?

Was there dramatic word emphasis?

Did the presenters employ appropriate movements/gestures?

What is the overall evaluation of the performance?

Chapter 8
Verbal Group Activities

By now your group has acquired the skills and confidence needed to begin work on group improvisation and other group activities. It's not that these are necessarily harder than the others, but group work can present its own challenges. The fact that these groups should be formed randomly and constantly reshuffled will mean that the group dynamics will change as well. Some members of the group will assert natural leadership qualities and will tend to take charge. This is not necessarily a bad thing because some of the others will tend to do better as followers. Whatever happens, the group work and resulting performances will be exciting to watch.

Because you are familiar by now with my suggestions about grouping, physical setup, distribution of topics, etc., I will not insult your intelligence by overdosing you with much more of the same in this last large section of the book. The general setup that I suggest for most of these activities is a straight line of chairs in front of the stage. Random groups of five or so would be best, so use the grouping technique appropriate for the number of participants you are working with. Have groups draw from a deck of cards to assign topics before starting planning time. Since many of these topics are more subjective, I'd suggest that you circulate to answer questions and give suggestions as needed (especially at the beginning). Then have the scenes presented in the order that they were assigned.

Scenes Based On ...

Who, What, Where?
Objective: Groups will be able to improvise a scene based on people, places, and situations.

Use the following situations to inspire scenes for groups.

Group #1

Place	People	Situation
In jail	prisoners, guards	all prisoners are due for release, but when the time comes …
Maternity ward	nurses, babies, visitors	conflict over mix-up of babies
Hell	the devil and new arrivals	the devil greets his guests
Carnival	carnies, carnival-goers	a paying customer uncovers crooked practices in the carnival games
Bar	customers, bartender	someone over the limit insists on more
Racetrack	bettors	people discuss their bets, but when the results are in …
Concert	performers, audience	performance is delayed and the audience gets restless
Donut factory	workers, boss	bored workers change the shape of the donuts
Fun house	friends, pranksters	one enters the fun house on a dare and others add to the fun
Department store	shoppers, sample distributors	people try to demonstrate their products on customers
Dungeon	victims, torturers	people are tortured for supposed crimes
Stadium	spectators, performers	conflict occurs between fans of opposing teams
Pet shop	animals, clerks, customers	clerks attempt to sell unusual pets
Deserted cabin	friends	they came to relax but find it hard work

Place	People	Situation
Airplane	crew, passengers	annoying habits cause conflicts
Funeral parlor	visitors, staff	something strange happens
Family reunion	family members	a will is about to be read and people are concerned
Fantasy island	hosts, visitors	will the fantasies come true?
Doctor's office	patient, doctor, receptionist	something is stuck in patient's ear and he demands immediate attention
Bank	customers, tellers	people are requesting too much cash and the tellers are in trouble
Hunting lodge	hunters, employees	after the day's hunt, a discussion of events occurs
Fast-food restaurant	job applicants, manager	manager finds fault with applicants
Pool hall	owner, customers	someone complains about a hustler
Subway station	passengers, security	train is late and people get impatient
School	students, teachers	students are cheating and try to avoid getting caught
Expensive restaurant	customers, waiter	some arrivals don't fit the normal clientele
Fish market	fishermen, customers	some are upset that bait machines don't operate properly
Comedy club	judges, contestants	comics compete for an award and the judges have to decide

Group #2:

Place	People	Situation
Jail cell	prisoners	planning to break out
Mountain cabin	married couple	held hostage by escaped convicts
Inside fence of concentration camp	prisoners	escaping
Porch of an old house	elderly people	chatting about the past
In an old building	variety of people	trying to survive a bombing
On a mountain top	mountain climbers	connected by ropes, scaling a mountain
Tenement building	unmarried pregnant girls	have to deal with the situation
Warden's office	social workers and warden	discussing a prisoner's request to be married before execution
Neighborhood	mail carrier	delivering mail on busy street
Empty circus tent	clowns	practicing act
Utility room	young children	helping with laundry
Backyard	children	meeting Martians
Tour bus	newlyweds	the brakes give out

Object, Animal, Place

Objective: Groups will be able to improvise a scene based on an object, an animal, and a place.

Use three equally numbered lists: one of objects, one of animals, and one of places. Form groups and have a member pick a number from one to fifteen (or whatever number your lists go to). Tell them privately what items are next to that number, and provide minimal planning time before groups perform the scenes. (Cross off used numbers as you go. If someone requests a used number, have them select again.)

Note: Since the items are very unrelated, be flexible and give credit for ingenuity.

Lists:

Objects

1. Marionette	6. Microwave	11. Flag
2. Fire hydrant	7. Swing	12. Suitcase
3. Chair	8. Roller coaster	13. Scissors
4. Statue	9. Car	14. Clock
5. Radio	10. Telephone	15. Burglar alarm

Animals

1. Cat	6. Elephant	11. Fish
2. Dog	7. Horse	12. Gerbil
3. Rabbit	8. Eagle	13. Tiger
4. Pigeon	9. Dragon	14. Gorilla
5. Duck	10. Bee	15. Hyena

Places

1. Prison	6. Bowling alley	11. Dark alley
2. Gas station	7. Dentist's office	12. Beach
3. Race course	8. Movie theatre	13. Dance club
4. Concert	9. At war	14. Playground
5. Insane asylum	10. Shoe store	15. Theme park

Places, Objects, People, Actions

Objective: Groups will be able to improvise a scene based on places, objects, people, and actions.

Follow the same procedure as in "Object, Animal, Place," using four lists instead of three.

Lists:

Places
1. Outer space
2. Cafeteria
3. Swimming pool
4. Cruise ship
5. Dark cellar
6. In a cave
7. At the hairdresser
8. Grocery store
9. Corner bar
10. Hotel lobby

Objects
1. Apple
2. Gun
3. Hammer
4. Book
5. Pipe
6. Ladder
7. Sweater
8. Money
9. Knife
10. Paper

People
1. Teenager
2. Bookworm (nerd)
3. Silly blond
4. Elderly grandmother
5. Salesperson
6. Sports nut
7. Model
8. Astronaut
9. Celebrity
10. Teacher

Actions
1. Jumping
2. Running
3. Shooting
4. Waving
5. Counting
6. Yelling
7. Cheering
8. Hitting (punching)
9. Spitting
10. Kissing

Situations

Objective: Groups will be able to improvise a scene based on situations.

Have groups create scenes from randomly selected situations.

Suggested Situations

Bet	Traffic accident
Special sale	Challenge
Class social experience	School disturbance
Looting	Gang fight
Natural disaster	Family disagreement
Surprise	Strange adventure
Mission	Debate

Person Speaking

Objective: Groups will be able to improvise a scene based on a person who is speaking for a reason.

Have groups create scenes from the ideas below.

Speeches

Doctor conducting group session about common problems
Soldier in charge making plans
Beautician to client, discussing makeup
Chef to waiter about service
Politician to followers about campaign
Student to classmates about school
Boss to employees about work
Cop to convicts about behavior
Babysitter to kids, discussing bedtime
Star to fans about career
Teacher to students about grades

What's Happening?

Objective: Groups will be able to improvise a scene based on randomly selected situations.

Have groups create scenes from the situations below.

Situations

Pompous minister is visiting the home of one of his congregation and finds fault with the things and people there.

Southern Belle causes jealous conflicts at an old-fashioned southern barbecue.

An overly protective parent refuses to leave his/her child at the mercy of school personnel.

Country hick is looking for work in a big city office building.

Society matron heads meeting to decide who can be admitted to a private country club.

Gangster meets with his/her cronies at a local Italian restaurant.

Dumb athlete reacts to pep talk by the coach before the big game.

New York chorus dancer greets various people in the dressing room right after the performance.

Little Mary Sunshine finds it hard to be appropriately sad at the funeral of an old classmate.

Where, What?

Objective: Groups will be able to improvise a scene based on activities and locations.

Have groups create scenes based on the activities and locations below.

Activities and Locations

Flying a kite in an open field during a storm
Catching a fish without a legal license
Building sand castles on a crowded beach
Picking a flower in a no-trespassing area
Lighting a cigarette in a no-smoking area
Taking a bath while other family members wait

Scenes Based on Places

People/Places

Objective: Groups will be able to improvise a scene based on people and places.

Have groups create scenes based on the following places and people.

Places and People

Place	People
Circus side show	performers, gypsies
Recording studio	performers, technicians
Graveyard	ghosts, goblins, grave diggers
Sewer	repairpersons, escaped convicts
Mine field	refugees, soldiers
Dark alley	winos, policepersons
Army mess hall	soldiers, cook
Top of building	jumper, tourists
Police station	cops, suspects
Cave	explorers, criminals
Top of mountain	hikers
Formal dining party	host, hostess
Beach	lifeguards
Carnival	concession clerk
City bus	passengers
Candy store	clerk
Used car lot	car dealer and customer
Jail	police officers
Cave	guide, tourists
Bowling alley	bowlers
Busy street	pedestrians
Park	joggers
Auction	auctioneer, bidders
Horse race	wealthy people
Prehistoric cave	cavemen and cavewomen
Soup kitchen	homeless people
Boardwalk benches	elderly people
Convention	salespeople
Comedy club	participants
Thrift store	shoppers

Place	People
Exercise club	members
Singles club	singles
Hospital ward	patients
Bar	drunks
Heaven or hell	recently deceased
The mall	teenagers
Library	librarians
Grocery store	shoppers
Funeral parlor	mourners
Fast-food restaurant	customers

You Are There

Objective: Groups will be able to improvise a scene based on given situations.

Have groups create scenes based on the following prompts. One person ("you" in the prompt) will begin the scene, then the rest of the group will join in.

Scene Prompts

You are losing in a card game. After careful observation, you decide someone is cheating.

You are playing "Santa," putting presents under the Christmas tree, when your children sneak downstairs and catch you.

You are making the bed and accidentally come across a sibling's diary.

You are at the swimming pool and the strict lifeguard is reprimanding you about breaking the rules.

You awake on Christmas morning to find all the presents missing.

A stranger at the amusement park sells you a fake pass to ride everything there.

You are in the supermarket with your troublesome children.

You fall asleep at the wheel of your car; when you wake up you find that you are dead and in heaven or hell.

You are playing pool when some tough guys demand to use the table.

You are camping out in the wilderness when someone claiming to be lost wanders up.

You answer a knock at the door and are confronted by a robber.

Where / Who?

Objective: Groups will be able to improvise a scene based on people and places.

Have groups create scenes based on the following prompts.

People and Places

Where	Who
Florist shop	plants, customers, workers
Public bus	passengers, driver, security
Political rally	candidates, followers
Opening of a play or movie	stars, critics, fans
Post office	packages, customers, workers
College orientation	teachers, students
Appliance store	appliances, customers, workers

Places / Happenings

Objective: Groups will be able to improvise a scene based on assigned situations.

Have groups create scenes based on the following prompts.

Group #1: Mix and Match

Places: dude ranch, large city zoo, shopping mall, circus, tourist trap
Happenings: humorous happening, conflict of forces, uncomfortable situation, revealing experience, frightening experience

Group #2: Assign as Listed

At the supermarket, a variety of people react to a slow, annoying person at the checkout.

At the carnival, a variety of people react to being cheated at a stand.

At the police station, a variety of people react to sharing a cell after a riot.

At the airport, various people react to an announcement that the flight is delayed.

In the school cafeteria, various students react to being assigned a table together.

In a restaurant, various people who are eating react to a smoker.

Place / Time / Theme

Objective: Groups will be able to improvise a scene based on places, times, and themes.

Have groups create scenes based on the following.

Place	Time	Theme
Park	early morning	never drink water
Bus station	3 AM	good conquers evil
All-night store	midnight	crime doesn't pay
Outside of church	dinner time	do unto others ...
Child's room	bedtime	once upon a time
In a theatre	during a live performance	make my day
Busy street corner	lunch time	love conquers all

Location, Location!

Objective: Groups will be able to improvise a scene based on locations.

Have groups create scenes based on locations.

Suggested Locations

On top of a tall building ready to jump
On a blind date
On a volcanic mountain when it erupts
Sleepwalking in your neighborhood
On an African safari
Appearing as a guest on a TV show
At a formal party dressed casually
At a rock concert where classical music begins to play
Having fallen into a shark-infested sea
Locked inside a dark house late at night
Camping during a natural disaster
Graveyard at midnight during a full moon
Beauty shop in expensive part of town
Boat far out in the ocean

Locker room of a sports team
In a school building at night without permission
Stall in a public restroom
Cave filled with bats
High-rise building during a fire
Closet in the home of a friend

Miscellaneous Places

Objective: Groups will be able to improvise a scene based on miscellaneous places.

Have groups create scenes based on the following prompts.

Group #1

Tree house	Mine	Attic
Dentist's office	Drug store	Saloon
Tower	Dormitory	Casino
Parking lot	Boxcar	Recording studio
Fashion show	Factory	Dungeon
Playground	Church	Cocktail lounge
Laundromat		

Group #2

Rock concert	Space ship	Bank
Football game	Cruise ship	Bookstore
Jungle	Beach	Woods
Retirement home	Auto repair shop	

Group #3

Preparing for skydiving	Hard day at the office
The heart of a big city	Small, closed-in room
A foreign country	Wedding
Basic training	Desert island
Traffic jam	Exclusive club
Junkyard	Ballet performance
Baseball game	Walk-in freezer
Inside a garbage truck	On top of a flag pole
On the roof of a school	At an engagement party
Inside a locked safe	Under a waterfall
Underneath a moving bus	At an ethnic festival
In an elevator	

Group #4
Payday at the unemployment office
At the travel agency
In the bingo hall
On the back porch

Scenes Based on Difficulties

Problems, Problems

Objective: Groups will be able to improvise a scene based on
        problems.

Have groups create scenes based on the following prompts.

Problem Situations
Parents insist that child comes along on family vacation but are later
        sorry.
Timid person is harassed by a gang until help arrives.
Employees are upset when boss's relative gets the position that one
        of them should have gotten.
Small children are affected by a powerful ad that they see on TV.
Students rebel when the authorities decide to lengthen the school
        day by two hours.
Kid's foolishness causes damage to parent's house.
Employee's foolishness causes customers to leave and management
        to complain.
Electricity goes out when children's parents are not home.

Variation
Provide a list of problem situations and give two possible ways to
end the scene. Groups should either decide which solution to use or
present two scenes which reflect both endings.

Example of Problems:
Woman is eight months pregnant with twins one year after the wedding.
Man is walking the floor with a screaming twin at three a.m.

Possible Solutions:
Person finds success/health in new life.
Person fails to overcome his/her problem and ...

Challenges

Objective: Groups will be able to improvise a scene based on challenges.

Have groups create scenes based on the following prompts.

Challenges

Timid teen is afraid to be alone in empty house at night.

Housewife decides life is boring and seeks a dramatic change.

Celebrity seeks to avoid recognition and have a normal day.

Elderly person seeks employment where mostly teens work.

Little child is left in the care of an irresponsible sitter.

Sophisticated lady invites unsophisticated new acquaintance to lunch.

Group of people visit a hypnosis clinic to stop smoking but are affected in strange ways.

Substitute teacher attempts to fill the shoes of a regular.

Young person finds out that he can have the trip of a lifetime if he can accomplish a difficult task.

Mother attempts to please her family by creating an unusual meal but is met with questionable success.

An inexperienced store clerk is approached by a variety of insistent customers.

Person has a flat tire while driving late at night through a rough neighborhood.

A contestant on a quiz show is nervous, and the host and other contestants aren't helping.

A social worker is investigating the home of unusual clients.

The operator of a day care center has a very different personality after the parents leave.

A special investigator for the IRS follows an anonymous report to check several people for fraud.

Surprise!

Objective: Groups will be able to improvise a scene based on unexpected situations.

Have groups create scenes based on the following prompts.

Unexpected Situations

A dating service connection proves interesting.

A trip to a glamorous place proves not-so-glamorous.

A wedding reception goes wrong.

A garage sale goes crazy.

A reunion proves embarrassing.

The opening of a new business goes less than smoothly.

A class expected to be dull proves to be anything but.

The purchase of an expensive item proves to be a waste of money.

A well-planned party does not go as planned.

Out of Control

Objective: Groups will be able to improvise a scene based on out-of-control situations.

Have groups create scenes based on the following prompts.

Suggested Situations

During lunch break downtown, people pour out of office buildings to crowd lunch rooms and shopping areas.

Kids are partying in a graveyard but things get out of control.

During a contest or sports event some fans' behavior gets out of hand.

A rotten, bratty kid causes trouble in a store and upsets his parents.

During a performance the audience acts up and upsets the performer.

A new employee has invited his new boss to dinner and family members complicate the experience.

People who are unable to go on a trip get the chance to ruin it for those who do.

A person who is out of control seeks help from a variety of sources.

Disaster

Objective: Groups will be able to improvise a scene based on disasters.

Have groups create scenes based on the following prompts.

Disasters

A seriously injured victim of a plane crash appeals for help but is not heard.

An old person sees his life's work destroyed by an earthquake.

A person is sentenced to life imprisonment for a crime he didn't commit.

Young people with similar injuries share their misery.

Confrontation

Objective: Groups will be able to improvise a scene based on confrontations.

Have groups create scenes based on confrontations.

Confrontations Between ...

... people of opposing views on a hot issue
... entertainer(s) and audience
... teacher(s) and student(s)
... police and criminals
... workers and management
... rich people and poor people

Complication

Objective: Groups will be able to improvise a scene based on complications.

Have groups create scenes based on the following prompts.

Complicated Situations

Place	Character	Complication
Airport	customers and terrorists	hijacking
Church	members and children	electric problem
Post office	clerks and customers	robbery
Bowling alley	bowlers and repairmen	breakdown
Bus station	customers and muggers	panic
Beauty shop	hairdresser and customers	fire

One Against

Objective: Groups will be able to improvise a scene based on one person up against a large group.

Have groups create scenes based on the following prompts.

Situations

Person	Situation
Millionaire	approached by many seeking financial help
Small child	trying to find lost parents in crowd
Elderly person	trying to get help from someone in an apartment building
Counselor	leading a difficult group session
Priest, minister	addressing hostile congregation
Soldier	approaching enemy village

Pressure

Objective: Groups will be able to improvise a scene based on high-pressure situations.

Have groups create scenes based on the following prompts.

Suggested Pressure Situations

Soldiers under attack
Spelunkers (cavers) 500 feet below
Police officers storming an armed building
Firefighters facing a blaze
Astronauts orbiting earth
Skydivers at 25,000 feet
Teachers on report card day
Camp counselors facing new arrivals
Politicians facing an angry crowd

Stressful

Objective: Groups will be able to improvise a scene based on stressful situations.

Have groups create scenes based on the following prompts.

Suggested Stressful Situations

Doctor misdiagnoses patient's ailment.
Shoe salesperson attempts to fit customer with wrong size.
Hairdresser botches customer's hair.
Passenger argues with cabbie about fare.
Soldier attacks incorrect target.
Waitperson serves customer wrong order.
Entertainer loses confidence in front of audience.
Robber makes serious mistake during theft.
Teacher takes students on overnight trip.
Fashion designer presents new line to the public.

Difficult

Objective: Groups will be able to improvise a scene based on difficult situations.

Have groups create scenes based on the following prompts.

Suggested Difficult Situations

Small child gets lost in a store and meets all kinds of people.
Homeless person goes to shelter to avoid freezing to death in the cold.
A haunted house party gets out of hand.
Teen runaway is taken to a group home by a social worker.
Person is arrested for shoplifting and taken to the police station.
Undercover cop in a school is found out and taken for a ride by angry students.
Wealthy child is kidnapped and held in an abandoned warehouse for ransom.
Small children go exploring and get locked in a closet.
Young person home alone on a stormy night watches a scary movie.
Group of people go for a roller coaster ride and get more than they bargained for.
Airplane develops engine trouble in flight.
Robbers attempt to break into a safe at night.
Rookie firefighters go out on their first call.

Annoyances of Life

Objective: Groups will be able to improvise a scene based on annoying situations.

Have groups create scenes based on the following prompts.

Suggested Annoying Situations

When outside mowing the lawn, you are approached by a neighbor complaining about the noise.

You sit in a non-smoking section, but a cigar smoker sits nearby.

You are moving into a new home, but your excitement fades when strange things begin to happen.

You are having so much fun playing in the woods that you don't realize you are lost.

When you settle into a seat at the movies, a strange person sits down next to you.

You are in nursery school, and strange things start to happen with the other children.

You are a member of a music group and think you are good enough to go out on your own, so you tell the others.

You are annoyed at being kept waiting for your appointment at the hairdresser.

You are walking your baby in the park, and someone claims that the child is his/hers.

You are at the doctor for a regular checkup, but the doctor has other ideas.

You are embarrassed that others in the school gym are so much better at the activities than you are.

You leave your machine at the laundromat to get a snack, and when you get back, someone has taken over the machine you were using.

Mistakes, Mistakes

Objective: Groups will be able to improvise a scene based on mistakes.

Have groups create scenes based on the following prompts.

Suggested Mistakes

While trying to repair a small leak, a plumber causes a major problem.

Airplane pilot miscalculates landing.

Counselor gives client the wrong advice.

Policeman attempts to apprehend the wrong person.

Scientist makes a brilliant discovery but loses credit.

Older people venture into a theatre not realizing that the films shown there are X-rated.

During the live filming of a TV soap, mistakes occur which must be covered up.

During the filming of a taste-test commercial, people keep picking the wrong brand.

Because of a need for money, a person accepts work as a servant for a snobby wealthy family.

Groups of vacationers are surprised by the joy ride to the hotel with a crazy bus driver.

Photographer out to make a name for himself takes sneaky pictures of people which they resent.

Owner of an art gallery replaces a painting by a famous artist with one done by a monkey to prove that art is a joke

Scenes Based on Contrast

Mood Reversal

Objective: Groups will be able to improvise a scene incorporating a mood reversal.

One participant sets the scene, and the second reverses the mood. Other group members fill in as needed.

Example Scenes

Character one is relaxing on an airplane flight when Character two calls the airline and says that he planted a bomb in Character one's carry-on.

Character one is relaxing by the family pool when Character two calls to report that a family member has been arrested.

Character one is watching TV at home when Character two calls to say that Character one's child has been expelled from school for drug possession.

Character one is jogging in the park when his cell phone rings and Character two says that he is watching Character one's every move.

Character one is relaxing in a local restaurant when Character two calls to say that Character one's roommate has left and taken all money and valuables.

Character one is relaxing at lunch when Character two calls to relate news of a death in the family.

Character one is asleep at home when a neighbor (Character two) calls to report someone is breaking into Character one's house.

Reactions

Objective: Groups will be able to improvise a scene based on reactions.

Groups relate scenes where various people react to the following prompts.

People React To ...

... a demanding boss
... a bank robbery
... a takeover by terrorists in a foreign land
... a flight delay
... a visitor from outer space
... an announcement of a 50% off sale for the next five minutes
... bag people
... a con-artist on a cruise ship looking for money

Reversal

Objective: Groups will be able to improvise a scene in which the mood of a situation is suddenly reversed.

Have groups create scenes based on the following prompts.

Reversal Situations

Family reunion becomes a feud.
Birthday party becomes a tragedy.
Long-awaited vacation turns into a nightmare.
Relative who has been away for a long time returns to family only to have been forgotten.
Outdoor cookout goes crazy when the grill explodes.
Formal dinner is a disaster when guests are poisoned.

Real-Life Situations

Objective: Groups will be able to improvise a scene based on real-life situations.

Groups create scenes which reflect themes of contrast and/or conflict.

Group #1

Themes:

Hard work vs. laziness   Respect vs. disrespect
Honesty vs. dishonesty   Socially in vs. out
Dumb vs. smart

Settings:

School   Work   Home
A club   A dance

Group #2

Beauty contestant looks for success but doesn't measure up.

Customer has high hopes but beautician fails to satisfy.

Person wins the lottery only to find he is sharing the winnings with many others.

Employee who expects a promotion is passed over for boss's relative.

Student who expects honor for outstanding achievement loses due to a technical error.

Group #3

Nervousness: You really like someone and have to meet his family.

Anger: You are invited to the wedding of someone you love and wanted to marry.

Overconfidence: You are an Olympic medal winner who has to retain the title.

Relaxation: You're overworked, but when you finally get vacation, you can't seem to wind down.

Surprise: You are the surprise at a surprise party.

Anger: You see some neighborhood kids outside vandalizing your house.

Pain: During a sports event you are injured and lose your chance for fame.

Fright: You are stranded in an elevator with a fear of small places.

Boredom: You pay to attend a concert but the star doesn't show and the replacement is lousy.

Confusion: You've been away from home for a long time and when you return, the reception is mixed.

Curiosity: You see someone relating a secret and are dying to know what it is.

Sorrow: You receive the news of the death of a friend but react strangely.

Unusual Situations

Objective: Groups will be able to improvise a scene based on unusual situations.

Have groups create scenes based on the following prompts.

Sample Unusual Situations

Monkeys in a jungle fail tree-climbing school.
Vampire in coffin is not thirsty for blood.
Persian cats at cat show don't want to be judged.
Santa Claus runs out of toys on Christmas Eve.
Child in the park has lost his balloon.
Skiers in Alps stuck on ledge.
Pilot's engine stops over the Bermuda Triangle.
Astronauts in space stray from the main ship and get lost.
Young girl at beauty show is there by mistake.
School personnel get together for a social outing.
Grounded teens try to sneak out.
Inexperienced waiters/waitresses are hired in a fancy restaurant.
Elderly people do some rugged bird watching.
College students meet on a cruise.
Mothers are tired of putting up with their kids.
Ex-Nazi in South America sees ex-victim.
Young child on the high-dive because of a dare.
Canoeists in the city sewer lost on a trip.

Opposites

Objective: Groups will be able to improvise a scene incorporating opposite character traits.

Have groups create scenes based on the following prompts.

Character Traits

Young vs. old at home
Energetic vs. lazy on the job
Strong vs. weak at camp
Outgoing vs. shy at a party
Conservative vs. artistic in a store
Brave vs. cowardly at war
Attractive vs. unattractive on the beach
Coordinated vs. klutzy in the gym

Incongruity

Objective: Groups will be able to improvise a scene incorporating incongruity.

Have groups create scenes based on the following prompts.

Incongruous Situations

Grandmotherly type at wrestling match
Muscular athlete at ladies' luncheon
Man buying ladies' clothes
Mother with children trying to handle packages
Lady in emergency trying to get help by phone
Society lady trying to deal with rodents
Tourist trying to instruct the guide

Scenes Based on Titles and Sayings

Titles

Objective: Groups will be able to improvise a scene based on a title.

Have groups create scenes inspired by these titles.

Group #1

Leisure and Luxury	Respect and Authority
Growing Old	Health and Happiness
To Be the Best	Adoption
Parent and Child	Drinking and Driving
Child Abuse	Truth and Justice
Working Mothers	Movie Mania
Drug Abuse	Raising Children
Careers and Salaries	College or Career?
Love and Marriage	

Group #2

The Submarine	The Sandbox
Substitute Teacher	Frozen Food
The Will	The Ugly Duckling
The Pet Shop	George Washington at Home
King Midas	Custer's Last Stand

Group #3

Day at the Beach	A Mixed-Up Mess
Trouble at School	Don't Throw Stones
Why Me?	A Video-Tape Experience
Fast-Food Frenzy	Picnic in the Park
Forever Friends	Kindergarten Days
Where Am I?	Nobody Cares
Vacation with the Family	Who Goes There?
Ready or Not, Here I Come!	Lights, Camera, Action!
Hospital Helpers	New Wardrobe
Share Your Troubles	Hint of Happiness
Where Does Love Go?	Rain, Rain, Go Away!
What's in a Name?	My Brother's Keeper

Group #4

On the Boardwalk
Used Car Lot
Day at the Cafeteria

Summer Job
At the Mall
The Hospital Experience

Group #5

Big Bully at School
Life's a Beach
Master and Slave
We Change with the Times
Music, Music, Music

In the Swim
Baby Trouble
It Takes All Kinds
Caught in the Trap

Group #6

Garbage Is Beautiful
Win at All Costs
The Stray Strangler
Slow But Steady

Life's a Jungle
The Black Cat
Never Give Up
It's How You Play the Game

Sayings

Objective: Groups will be able to improvise a scene based on common sayings.

Have groups create scenes inspired by these sayings.

Group #1

The shoe's on the other foot.
It cuts both ways.
Think before you act.
Better late than never.
The clothes make the man.
Do unto others as you would have them do unto you.
Be the best you can be.
Money is the root of all evil.
Enjoy yourself — it's later than you think.
Don't worry; be happy.
You can't judge a book by its cover.
Faith can move mountains.
Honor your father and mother.
Time waits for no man.
Sing for your supper.
Love makes the world go 'round.
Practice makes perfect.

Time marches on.
Go for it.
Live life to the fullest.
Practice what you preach.
One man's trash is another man's treasure.
Just say no.
If at first you don't succeed, try, try again.
Don't give up the ship.
It takes two to tango.
Never say die.

Group #2

Save up for a rainy day.
You're only as old as you feel.
The pen is mightier than the sword.
Say no to drugs.
It's never too late.
It's later than you think.
Loose lips sink ships.
Be true to yourself.
Reach for the stars.
Be grateful for what you have.
Think positively.

Group #3

Life's too short.
A penny saved is a penny earned.
Waste not, want not.
Love your neighbor.
No pain, no gain.
You can lead a horse to water, but you can't make him drink.
Birds of a feather flock together.
When it rains, it pours.

Scenes Based on Senses

Smells

Objective: Groups will be able to improvise a scene based on smells.

Have groups create scenes based on the following prompts.

Smells

Smoky smell of a fire
Smell of newly mowed lawn
Overpowering odor of strong perfume
Smell of chlorine bleach
Odor of spices
Body odor
Gasoline fumes
Exhaust fumes
Scent of fresh flowers
Smell of rotten cabbage
Smell of freshly baked bread

Tastes

Objective: Groups will be able to improvise a scene based on tastes.

Have groups create scenes based on the following prompts.

Tastes

Turkey with stuffing
Steamed crabs
Broccoli and cauliflower
Steak
Hamburgers

Popcorn
Asparagus
Pecan pie
Scrambled eggs

Sounds

Objective: Groups will be able to improvise a scene based on sounds.

Have groups create scenes that incorporate one or more of the following sounds.

Group #1

Knocking	Bells ringing	Whispering
Screaming	Traffic noise	Boat whistle
Drum beat	Singing	

Group #2

Explosion	Gunshot	Hammering
Horn honking	Gum cracking	Humming
Wind blowing	Insects buzzing	Siren wailing
Groaning	Door creaking	Engine running
Infant crying	Slaps	Footsteps
Telephone ringing	Hysterical laughter	Echo
Pounding	Counting	

Miscellaneous Senses

Objective: Groups will be able to improvise a scene based on various sense-related situations.

Have groups create scenes based on the following prompts.

Sensory Prompts

Person who has lost the ability to speak is misunderstood.
Person who is paralyzed asks someone to describe a sensation.
Deaf person has difficulty understanding directions.
Blind person tries to rely on other senses to travel to work alone.
Person without the sense of smell needs help selecting perfume.
Person with ESP makes unusual predictions.
Person unable to taste finds fault with food served.

Scenes Based on TV

Eyewitness Reports

Objective: Groups will be able to improvise a scene structured around an eyewitness report at a given scene.

Have groups create eyewitness reports based on the following situations.

Eyewitness Situations

At a fire	At the scene of an accident
At a demonstration	After a mugging
During a riot	

Stereotypes

Objective: Groups will be able to improvise a scene incorporating stereotypes that go along with a given prompt.

Have groups create scenes based on the following prompts.

Stereotypical Prompts

Hospital	Soap opera
Cowboy/Indian	Crime
Mystery/detective	Family sitcom
Game show	Talk-show
News	Interview
Travel/lifestyle	Disaster/reaction
Adventure/nature	Love/romance

News

Objective: Groups will be able to improvise a news scene.

Have groups create newsroom scenes based on the following prompts.

News Shows

The Old-Folk News (senior citizen)
The Tiny-Tot News (little kid)
The Teen-Scene News (13-19)
The Down-Home News (country)
The With-It News (big city)
The Upbeat News (rock and roll)

Popular Shows

Objective: Groups will be able to improvise a scene based on popular shows.

Have groups create parodies/imitations of popular TV shows. Scenes should feature typical characters, actions, plots, etc.

Show Title and Type

Group #1:

Success to the Strong (physical challenge)
Love in the Afternoon (soap)
Terror on the Beach (horror)
Fantasy of the Stars (celebrity)
Loyalty to the End (news)
Embarrassment of All Time (talk)
Confusion among the Ranks (comedy)
Revenge of the Unexpected (game)
Challenge at the Races (sports)
Complication to the Max (game)
Fun in the Sun (exercise)
How's It Goin'? (sitcom)

Group #2:

Let's Do It (hobby or craft)
Athlete's Showcase (sports)
Voice Over (talk)
PS #211 (school)
Under 10 (children's)
Bottoms Up (food)

The Bet's the Limit (game)
It's Show Time (variety)
Question of Guilt (mystery)
What's New? (fashion)
Branches of Life (soap)

Group #3:

Quest for Dreams (game)
Before It's Too Late (suspense)
Only Friends (sitcom)
Only the Three of Us (sitcom)
Come Stretch with Me (exercise)
Straight from the Heart (talk)
High School Heat (news)
It's in the Bag (game)

Love Triangle (soap)
Today's People (talk)
Cooking with Simplicity (food)
Chicago Beat (police)
Trouble at Big Gulch (western)
Way Out (sci-fi)
City Streets (police)

Group #4:

Eyes on the World (news)	Believe It or Not (sitcom)
Inside Our USA (special)	Toast of the Town (talk)
Case of the Dead Canary (mystery)	Life in the Fast Lane (game)
Parade of Values (game)	World Class Winners (talk)
Be All You Can Be (special)	Midnight Magic (suspense)

Group #5:

It Cuts Both Ways (drama)	It Takes a Criminal (crime)
Little Red School House (children's)	Wish Upon a Star (game)
To Be the Best (sports)	Life with the Homeless (expose)
Guns and Saddles (western)	I Wonder (children's)
Under the Knife (medical)	Upbeat (music)
Meet Me (talk)	Wise Acré (sitcom)

Sequential Scenes

Sequence

Objective: Groups will be able to improvise a scene with various components happening in sequential order.

Divide into groups (number dependent on each selection). Assign one of the stages of the sequence to each group. After planning time is provided, have the scenes presented in sequential order.

Age

Young children: "She Hit Me First"
Elementary: "The Fire Drill"
Early teens: "Goodbye Grandma"
Junior High: "The Bargain"
Teenage: "I Thought You Were My Friend"
Late teens: "Last Chance"
Young adult: "Three Kleenex Movies"
Grown up: "Beauty for Sale"
Elderly: "They'll Be Sorry When I'm Gone"

Vacation

Planning the trip
Packing for the trip
En route
The welcome/arrival
Reunion at dinner

Cleaning up
Thank you/good-bye
Discussing the trip/returning home
Arrival home

Love

Love at first sight
The engagement
The wedding
First anniversary

Birth of baby
Baby's first steps
(more can be added here)
Golden wedding anniversary

Reunion

First time this group met
This group engaged in a typical activity
Members of this group in separate lives after leaving group
This group reuniting 10 years after disbanding

Life

First day at school
Entering middle school
Beginning high school
First date

Learning to drive
Senior prom
Graduation
First day on the job

Before and After

The way they were in school ....Class reunion
Dorm mates......................................After 20 years
When they first moved in ....After several years
The happy wedding day ....The divorce

Seasonal Scenes

These scenes can be coordinated around various holidays/ celebrations.

Halloween

Objective: Groups will be able to improvise a scene based on Halloween-related prompts.

Have groups create scenes based on the following prompts.

Halloween Situations

Several people gather to watch scary movies.
Child rebels against babysitting brother/sister.
Small children trick-or-treat for the first time.
Home owner makes unusual plans for Halloween night.
Teenagers (too old to do so) go trick-or-treating.
Children help parents dress up for Halloween.
Small child asks questions about Halloween.
At a costume party it is difficult to tell what's real from what's unreal.

Thanksgiving

Objective: Groups will be able to improvise a scene based on Thanksgiving-related prompts.

Have groups create scenes based on the following prompts.

Thanksgiving Situations

You arrive for Thanksgiving too early.
You are delayed in the airport trying to get home for Thanksgiving.
You eat too much Thanksgiving dinner.
Someone arrives for Thanksgiving who wasn't invited.
The TV stops working (no football).
Family arguments occur over Thanksgiving dinner.
You have to prepare the entire Thanksgiving meal for thirty people.

Snow

Objective: Groups will be able to improvise a scene based on snow-related prompts.

Have groups create scenes based on the following prompts.

Winter Prompts

A place that rarely gets snow experiences its pleasures.
Little kids build snow forts and have a snowball fight.
Traffic accidents abound due to slick streets.
Snow sports abound due to a fresh covering.
A family gets stuck in their car during a snowstorm.
A surprise snow strands a group in a wilderness cabin.
A special date is ruined due to snow.
School is dismissed early due to snow.

Christmas

Objective: Groups will be able to improvise a scene based on Christmas-related prompts.

Have groups create scenes based on the following prompts.

Christmas Situations

A visiting relative gets drunk and falls into the Christmas tree.
Shoppers return to their car to find that their purchases have been stolen.
Parents who are poor have to make the best for the children.
Family traveling out of town gets stranded in a blizzard before arrival.
A person becomes very depressed over the coming holiday.
A little child visits Santa to ask for special gifts.
While caroling in the neighborhood, children find a strange house and people.
A family gathering for the holidays changes from happy to ...
A small child falls asleep on Christmas Eve and dreams his toys come to life.
A person spends extra time selecting the perfect gift for a friend, but ...

Scenes Based on Age

Childhood

Objective: Groups will be able to improvise a scene based on childhood-related prompts.

Have groups create scenes based on the following prompts.

Brats

In a department store, a child wants every toy.

At an amusement park, a child wants to go on every ride.

At a playground, a child wants his parent to share every piece of equipment.

In church, a child wants to play and won't keep quiet.

In a restaurant, a child wants special food and won't eat.

In a grocery store, a child wants candy.

A child follows younger children around and bullies them.

Kids

Because of a power failure, school is closed, and kids return home while parents are still working.

Kids are dropped off at school by their parents, but they decide not to stay there.

A bunch of kids get bored being home on vacation and …

Kids from different backgrounds are forced to live and work together at a camp.

School

Objective: Groups will be able to improvise a scene based on school-related prompts.

Have groups create scenes based on the following prompts.

You Are …

… a 7th grader walking past the 9th grade lockers between classes.

… a sophomore on the first day of school in a class comprised mostly of seniors and juniors.

… 5 years old and entering kindergarten for the first time.

… leaving your 2nd grade class on the last day of school.

… a 9th grader walking past the 7th grade lockers between classes.

… a senior walking to class when you see someone you'd like to ask out but are too shy.

Report Card

Parents have to decide what to do about child's poor grades.

Teacher deliberately fails a student because he is a behavior problem.

Parents doubt the authenticity of child's report card.

Child hesitates to bring home a very poor report card.

Student objects to a poor grade and goes to complain to the teacher involved.

Prom

Use an announcer/commentator to give the song titles of each of these sequential scenes about prom:

"Break It to Me Gently" — asking for a date

"Happy Days Are Here Again" — making plans

"Rock Around the Clock" — the dance starts

"Save the Last Dance for Me" — the dance is nearly over

"The Party's Over" — saying goodnight

"Memories" — looking back

Use the following to inspire group scenes concerning prom:

Guy/girl starts flirting with someone else's date.

Guy and girl split up right before the prom, but go together anyway.

Guy finds he is unable to pay for all the expenses.

A disagreement occurs among friends sharing a limo en route.

Waiter/waitress gives kids a hard time at pre-prom dinner.

Girl goes shopping for prom outfit.

The post-prom party gets out of hand.

Guy has to work up nerve to ask someone to the prom.

It's prom night and everything seems to go wrong.

It's prom night and it seems like a dream come true.

Teachers

Have each group create a scene about a specific teacher from the assigned department without ridiculing or making fun of that person.

Industrial Arts	Business	Guidance
Math	English	Home-Ec
Phys. Ed.	Science	Social Studies
Foreign Language		

Elderly

Objective: Groups will be able to improvise a scene based on age-related prompts.

Have groups create scenes, incorporating elderly characters, based on the following prompts.

Situations

Meeting in the park
In a retirement home
On a seniors' bus trip
At the supermarket
Shopping for clothes
Listening to music
Watching TV
In the park

Waiting for the doctor
At a dance for seniors
At a dinner for seniors
Visiting with friends
Giving advice to the young
In a hospital
Crossing the street

Scenes Based on Visual Sources

Pictures

Objective: Groups will be able to improvise a scene based on pictures.

Gather a large number of pictures from discarded magazines (try to select those showing a limited number of people in some kind of emotional setting). Form groups and assign (or have them select) a picture to each group. Allow plan time to have them develop scenes inspired by their pictures. Present each scene. Circulate the corresponding picture in the audience after each scene is presented.

Comics

Objective: Groups will be able to improvise a scene based on comics.

Clip a number of comic strips from discarded newspapers.

Form groups and assign (or have them select) a comic strip to each group. Allow plan time and have them either act out the strip or portray the character(s) in some way. Following each performance, pass around the corresponding strip in the audience.

Note: Every group member must participate even if they must be objects in the scene.

Play Summaries

Objective: Groups will be able to improvise a scene based on play summaries.

Cut out a number of short play summaries from play catalogs. Form groups and assign (or have them select) a play summary to each group. Allow plan time for them to create a scene inspired by the summary. They should use something (a character, the title, the theme, etc.) from the summary as a basis. Following each performance, pass around the corresponding play summary to the audience.

Miscellaneous Activities

Words

Objective: Groups will be able to improvise a scene based on series of words.

Each group gets a series of related words to create a scene.

Notes: Consult a thesaurus for additional material. This activity can provide an entertaining way to increase vocabulary skills.

Word Series

Gibberish, meaningless or unintelligent talk
Deck, fix up, primp
Fiend, devil, Beelzebub, Satan
Imperative, masterful, bossy, domineering
Betrothed, engaged, contracted
Juncture, connection, coupling, joining
Compulsion, clamor, tumult, upheaval
Precipitate, deposit, abrupt, hasty, sudden
Masher, wolf, chaser, lady-killer
Oust, cast out, deport, expel
Quiescent, dormant, lurking, potential
Heist, steal, snitch, swipe
Sensationalist, livid, lurid, sultry
Scamp, rascal, rogue, villain
Repulse, keep off, repel, ward off
Nutty, buggy, keen, jealous
Libel, defame, scandalize, slander
Elite, choice, prime, pride
Adroitness, deftness, dexterity, readiness

Emotions

Objective: Groups will be able to improvise a scene based on emotional situations.

Have groups create scenes based on the following prompts.

Emotional Situations

Actress is frustrated because of an inability to learn lines.

Employee is angry when boss keeps assigning dirty jobs.

Hairdresser is nervous because he lacks experience with difficult customers.

Teacher is angry when student tells him how to conduct class.

Waiter is annoyed with flirtatious customers.

Police officer is scared when faced with life-threatening situations.

New apartment dweller is angry with landlord about roaches, rats, etc.

Repair-person is disgusted at having to work on filthy appliances.

Patient is anxious as he waits to see the doctor.

Customer is disgusted when every piece of clothing he tries on looks terrible.

Detective remains determined to solve a murder case even when attempts to distract him abound.

Person is embarrassed to have to shop for a used car with very limited funds.

Person is so anxious to get rich that he uses questionable methods.

A very intelligent person is too proud to accept help with a difficult challenge.

Normally Non-Speakers

Objective: Groups will be able to improvise a scene incorporating characters who normally don't speak.

Groups are assigned the following prompts and create scenes where the normally non-speaking characters communicate with one another. It is understood that these conversations are not overheard by the "real world."

Non-Speakers

Newborn babies in a hospital nursery

Toys in a toy shop

Appliances in a kitchen

Products on a shelf in a grocery store

Animals in a pet shop
Items of clothing in a department store
Plants in a garden
Pieces of furniture in a room

Communication Scenes

Objective: Groups will be able to improvise a scene based on communication.

Group #1

a. Create a scene in which two groups must communicate over a great distance, keeping vocal contact realistic and suggestive of the distance.

Example: Guides and lost tourists in a cave

b. Create a scene in which two groups must communicate in close proximity, being restricted to whispering only (stage whispers must be loud enough to be heard by the audience).

Example: People being held captive

Group #2

Groups are assigned topics which concern difficult communication situations and have to create appropriate scenes.

Topics:

You tell your parents that you are marrying a person twice your age.

You tell the police officer that stopped you for speeding that you refuse to accept the ticket.

You tell someone a very dirty joke, and they are offended.

You attempt to communicate the answers to a test to someone while the teacher is in the room.

You have to tell a close friend that you are moving out of town.

You break down on a lonely highway and have to convince someone to give you a lift.

You try to communicate to get a deaf person out of danger.

You try to pass secret information to a prisoner in an observed visiting situation.

While talking to a wrong-number caller, you discover something special about him/her.

While in a foreign country, you try to get directions from a native.

You are forced to lie to your parents, and they do not believe you.

You must tell someone that he has an incurable disease.

You have to tell an employee that he is fired because of bad breath.

113

Famous Movie Scenes

Objective: Groups will be able to improvise a scene based on famous movie scenes.

Select or assign famous movies to each group. Have each develop scenes from the selection.

Possible Movies

A Christmas Carol   *The Wizard of Oz*

E.T.   *King Kong*

Gone With the Wind

Come Together:

Objective: Groups will be able to improvise a scene based on situations in which people come together.

Have groups develop scenes from the following situations.

Suggested Prompts

Prisoners join forces to escape.

Strangers end up in a lifeboat after their ship sinks.

Students from different schools meet at an overnight conference to discuss problems.

A number of people arrive at the same time to be interviewed for the same job.

During an emergency, a number of people are evacuated to safety in a shelter.

Vacationers who start out as strangers develop relationships.

Shoppers in a grocery store join forces to protest high prices.

Kids of various ages in the same neighborhood put aside differences to get even with grouchy neighbors.

Patients in a hospital find out that they have been overcharged and come together to remedy the situation.

Employees from various backgrounds plan a campaign to get salaries raised.

Homeless people seek shelter from the cold on a warm subway and refuse to leave when the police intervene.

Clothing

Objective: Groups will be able to improvise a scene based on clothing.

List a large variety of items of clothing and assign each group one or more to use as a basis for a scene.

Note: The actual items can be provided for use if possible.

Possible items of clothing: Large sweater and turtleneck, full-length mink coat, etc.

Charges

Objective: Groups will be able to improvise a scene based on situations involving charges and demands.

Group 1: In Charge

Have groups develop scenes from the following situations where one person is in charge of a group of others.

Sample Situations:

Adult in charge of small children at the zoo
Teacher in charge of students on a field trip
Cruise director in charge of passengers on vacation
Guard in charge of convicts on a chain gang
Landlord in charge of college students who room in his house
Tour director in charge of seniors on a bus trip

Group 2: Demands

Have groups develop scenes from the following situations where someone makes a charge or a demand.

Sample Situations:

A student denies a charge of cheating when accused.
A young person promises to be careful when requesting the use of a car.
A friendly discussion develops into an argument.
A parent demands that his son be excused from a class.
A teacher demands for the thousandth time that a student not talk in class.
A customer demands to handle a very expensive necklace.
A customer demands that the clerk get an item from the top shelf and then doesn't want it.

A young person insists that a classmate is not as nice as everyone thinks.

A person demands to see his best friend who has been rushed to the hospital.

Election Scenes

Objective: Groups will be able to improvise a scene based on elections.

Have groups develop scenes from the following situations involving elections.

Election Situations

A scandal occurs during your campaign.

You are in the middle of a campaign speech when ...

An important candidate is kidnapped.

While campaigning, you find out that your spouse is an alcoholic.

You are debating your opponent on a controversial issue.

You are the child of a candidate and ...

You react to hearing that you've won/lost the election.

Firsts

Objective: Groups will be able to improvise a scene based on firsts.

Have groups develop scenes from the following situations which involve firsts.

Firsts

First accident

First fight

First day of marriage

First day on the job

First day divorced

First day at school

First day as a parent

What Happens After

Objective: Groups will be able to improvise a scene based on given situations.

Have groups develop scenes from the following situations.

What happens after ...

... the performance?   ... school?
... the family reunion?   ... the divorce?
... the wild party?   ... the catastrophe?

Group Involvement Scenes

First Liners Revisited

Objective: Students will be able to jump into a group scene that begins with a pair of participants holding a conversation based on a line they were given.

If you need to, go back and review the procedure for "First Liners" that appears at the beginning of Chapter 7. Follow the same directions for setup, etc. Use some of the same starting lines, or make up new ones. Begin as usual with a pair of participants in the middle of the circle having a conversation built from the original line.

Mandatory Jump-Ins

During the course of the conversation, another person is sent into the scene, and he must become a part of the conversation/action in a logical manner. Select one of the following variations to involve other members of the group.

Leader Directed

When the group is seated in a circle of chairs watching a pair of participants speaking in the center, the leader should approach someone seated in the circle from behind. Indicate with a tap on the shoulder that they are to enter the scene in progress. If they look puzzled about what to do, whisper a quick suggestion to help. They then enter the scene with a line of their choosing, and the scene progresses until you send in another person or end the scene. This method allows you to observe and make assessments about who is the most comfortable entering the scene.

In Sequence

Follow exactly the same procedure as in Leader Directed, except have the participants enter the scene in the order in which they are seated in the circle (rather than entering when directed by you). They should know when it is their turn and make their entrance as soon after the scene begins as possible. The scene will end when you call "Curtain." You may choose to let the scene continue long enough for more than one person to join the original pair, or you may end the scene with only three participants.

Jump-In Situations

Objective: Students will be able to jump in (or make a phone call in) to a group scene that begins with one person who takes his designated place in a specific setting.

Notes: Although the setup and manner of starting the scene is different from "First Liners," the involvement of the members of the group is similar. This is one of the more complicated activities included in the book, and it is also one of the most popular.

If you do not have a ringing device to signal a phone call in to the scene, simply call out "Ring, ring," to indicate it.

The following activities should involve all or most of the participants, although not equally. After setting the stage for the start of the scene, there are three ways to add and remove participants from the scene in progress. The person in charge should orchestrate an appropriate ending rather than having an abrupt conclusion based on a time limit. An example will be provided to illustrate possibilities.

Starting the Scene

Divide the space you are using into a seating/audience area for most of the participants and a large acting area (Be sure that participants are able to flow easily from one area to the other. There should be no barriers between the two).

Decide what the setting will be for the scene and set the acting area up with representative furniture and props.

Select participants to begin the scene and have them take appropriate positions in the acting area.

Describe the setting and the identity of the starters to all participants, indicating the purpose of any props and furniture. Include a prop telephone to allow outside communication into the scene while in progress.

When ready to begin, have the designated starters perform some appropriate actions. Almost immediately other participants will move into the scene via one of the following methods.

1. Directed

The easiest and less chaotic method is at your direction. When you deem it appropriate, quietly whisper to a person in the audience area what his identity/function will be and send him into the scene in progress. Phone calls in to the scene can also be directed. You may indicate when the person being sent in should exit, or you can "phone calls" for this purpose.

2. Mandatory

The participants in the audience area can be numbered or positioned in some order. At an appropriate time (on a signal from you) the next person in order must enter the scene. If he can't come up with a logical identity/function on his own, he should quickly and quietly seek your help.

3. Voluntary

The most adventurous (and often chaotic) method is allowing participants to flow in and out of the scene without involvement from you. This method favors the more aggressive participants, and is therefore not the most democratic method. There is also a tendency to overstay on the part of those who like to volunteer, therefore a time limit for each volunteer joining the scene should be announced before starting.

Example of a Jump-In Situation:

Setting: Classroom (teacher's desk, classroom desks, chairs, chalkboard, etc.) The starter is designated as the teacher in the classroom before the class arrives (straightening up, writing on the board, etc.).

Characters to be added/removed: Various students, the principal, the school nurse, a parent, a custodian, other teachers, etc.

Possible telephone calls to come in: Parents, bomb scare, wrong number, crank caller, friend of student, etc.

Logical endings: Ringing of the bell, evacuation of the building, end of the school day, etc.

Possible Settings and Characters:

Setting	Characters
Car wash	manager, attendant
Boardwalk	pedestrian, cop
Resort	visitor, con-artist
Ballpark	fan, vendor
Prom	student, band member
Store	customer, clerk
Unemployment office	applicant, clerk
Bank	teller, manager
Play rehearsal	director, cast member
Retirement home	resident, visitor
Day care center	owner, child
Church	minister, member
Funeral parlor	director, mourner
Movie theatre	usher, attendee
School hall	student, teacher
Bus	driver, passenger
Restaurant	waiter, customer

Word Association

Objective: Students will be able to repeat as many previously stated words as possible before adding one to the chain.

Form a large circle with all participants standing if front of chairs. Select a person to act as starter and have him say a word aloud. Proceed in a clockwise direction with each person repeating aloud the previous word(s) and then adding another which in some way associates with the previous words. Participants who make a mistake or are unable to continue are eliminated and will be seated. Continue this procedure until time is up or the number of words accumulated becomes too difficult to remember.

Notes: The words should not form sentences. Improper words are not acceptable. Be careful not to offend participants who are not as capable as others.

This can be a difficult activity for some, so be careful not to make it a contest. Used correctly, this is good practice for memorization.

Student-Directed

Objective: Students will be able to volunteer to direct others in an original scene or participate in a scene involving other group members.

This is one of the rare exceptions to the rule about random grouping. You will be allowing your student directors to select their own casts. Since the group members have been working together so long, this will hopefully present no problem.

Ask for volunteers to determine persons to direct scenes.

Student directors create a scene and select casts.

Note: If you wish, you can have several directors at once. Let the first one select his cast and go to a planning area with them. Then have the next director select from the remaining students. Continue until all students have been cast.

On Trial

Objective: Students will be able to work in a group to plan and participate in a kind of mock trial.

Method #1

Working in groups, students complete "On Trial" plan sheet and decide who will play which parts (judge, the accused, defense and prosecuting attorneys, witnesses).

Planning time is provided and trials are presented.

"On Trial" Plan Sheet:

The crime (give details): _____

When? _____

Where? _____

The accused (give motives): _____

Witnesses:

— For _____

— Against _____

The verdict (if there is no jury, judge will decide guilt or innocence):

_____

Method #2

This method requires four persons per group. The judge states who is accused and of what, the prosecutor gives reasons the accused is guilty, the defense gives reasons the accused is not guilty, and the accused tells his side. The judge (or audience) gives verdict and his reasons behind his decision.

Possible Trials:

Young person accused of lying

Person accused of speeding

Woman accused of witchcraft

Soldier accused of treason

Person accused of murder

Crime Stoppers

Objective: Students will be able to work in a group to plan and participate in a scene where a detective interviews suspects to solve a crime.

Each group completes a "Crime Stoppers" plan sheet. The group assigns someone to be the detective; all others are suspects.

Scenes are presented where the detective interviews each suspect and the real criminal is revealed.

"Crime Stoppers" Plan Sheet:

Title: _____

The crime (give details): _____

Who did it: _____

The motive: _____

List of suspects and their possible motives: _____

Piece of evidence which reveals the true criminal: _____

Man on the Street

Objective: Students will be able to participate in a group to create scenes based on interviews.

Establish four or more groups with one participant interviewing the rest of the participants in the group.

Possible Situations

Interviewing elderly people

Interviewing children

Interviewing talking animals

Interviewing students at school

Job Interviews

Objective: Students will be able to participate in a group to create scenes based on interviews.

Establish groups with one participant designated as a person being interviewed for a job and the others designated as the interviewing panel.

Possible Interviews

A substitute being interviewed by a group of teachers

An entertainer being interviewed by the owners of a fancy resort

An actor being interviewed by the executive staff of a film

Someone who has done a heroic deed being interviewed by a number of journalists

A clergy member being interviewed by a number of religious persons

A babysitter being interviewed by a group of wealthy parents

A possible candidate for political office being interviewed by members of the candidate's political party

Sculptures

Objective: Students will be able to participate in a group scene incorporating human sculpture.

Use the circle setup with the PA in the center. If you want everyone to have a chance to be a creator, list all of the participants' names on cards and repeat the activity several times, drawing a card for the new creator until all have been used.

One person "sculpts" two other people into a position. When the sculpture is complete, the creator claps his hands to indicate that the scene should begin.

The sculpted pair must create a scene with a beginning, middle, and end based on their opening positions. The creator may say "freeze" at any time during the scene to halt the action, at which point the pair will hold the position until instructed to continue. The creator may send in another participant to take the position of either person during a freeze, and then the action will continue.

Continue in this manner until the scene reaches its conclusion.

Choral Chant

Objective: Students will be able to participate in a group as either the director or a member of the chorus in order to produce a choral chant.

Compile a selection of very familiar songs ("Happy Birthday," etc.). Select a choral director for each group and assign a song.

The director should arrange his group and lead them in a practice session of chanting the words to the song. The director should change the speed and volume several times and direct an appropriate closing.

Presentations are given when groups are ready.

Post Office

Objective: Students will be able to participate in a group scene as either employees or customers in a post office setting.

Assign three postal clerk parts: Irritable but efficient, slow-moving and good at avoiding work, new and temporary on the job. Have these three characters establish the scene and open the post office doors.

Assign other characters to enter the scene, giving a signal to each when it is time to enter. These characters will exit the scene when their assigned task has been completed.

Possible Entry Characters

An old person who wants to talk to everyone (even himself)

Person in a hurry to mail packages, wrapping them while standing in line

Successful lawyer who came to pick up an important package which is now missing

A rich snob who needs to buy stamps but is disgusted with the other people in the post office

A vagrant who has no real business besides wanting to come inside out of the weather

A child whose parents are divorced wants to send a letter to dad but is five cents short

A middle-aged person who is in a hurry to mail packages tries to bribe an employee to get faster service.

A volunteer worker who is trying to get customers to sign a petition

A plain-clothes detective tailing a murder suspect he thinks is there

Note: This activity can be easily reused by selecting a different setting for the employees and customers. Be sure to have enough characters to match the number of participants you wish to involve.

Chapter 9
Written Activities

Although theatre activities are mainly physical and verbal, you may find some use for related written activities. I have not included objectives for these, but I'm sure that you could create appropriate ones if you feel the need to do so.

Individual

Issues and ideas

Each student writes down the following information.

(Note: Except for the last item, the responses to each item should be related.)

1. Draw a symbol.
2. Write a controversial statement.
3. Identify a real person (past or present).
4. Write your opinion of the statement and person.
5. Name two fellow participants.

Application: Author joins with the two participants named to direct a scene having to do with what he wrote on the card.

Invent a Character

Each student lists the following information about an imaginary character.

1. Sex	7. Occupation
2. Age	8. Physical condition
3. Name	9. Attitude
4. Height	10. Likes/dislikes
5. Weight	11. Other important details
6. Hair color	

Applications: Students can portray characters in whatever scenes they are working on.

Create a Character

Students list the following information which is later used to portray a character:

1. A color	7. An article of clothing
2. A first name	8. A number
3. A city	9. A nationality
4. A type of car	10. A sport
5. A level of education	11. An occupation
6. A kind of food	12. A beverage

Applications: Same as in "Invent a Character."

Play Review

Each student selects a play to read or view. Then he completes as much of the following outline as possible based on the play.

Note: The vocabulary included in the outline should be studied/reviewed prior to the assignment.

1. Title and author
2. Exposition:
   a. Time
   b. Place
   c. Mood/atmosphere
   d. Preliminary situation
3. Plot:
   a. Initial incident
   b. Rising action
   c. Climax
   d. Falling action
   e. Conclusion (final outcome for each major character)
4. Characters: (describe each in a sentence)
   a. Protagonist
   b. Antagonist
   c. Secondary
   d. Minor characters (list only)
5. Theme (state in one sentence)
6. Personal reaction (your honest opinion of the play)
7. Quotation (one or more important lines/passages)

Individual or Pair

Writing an Incredibly Short Play

Students working either individually or in pairs are instructed to complete a plan sheet (see below). Then they will use separate paper to write their short play using correct play form.

Plan Sheet

(Allow space when preparing the plan sheet for student responses.)

Title: _____

Setting
Time: _____

    Place: _____

    Atmosphere: _____

Main character

    Name: _____

    Description: _____

Conflict
Main character vs.: _____

Circumstances which involved main character in conflict:

_____

_____

How conflict is resolved (ended): _____

Other characters involved (optional):

_____

Play Format

Title/author(s)

List cast (in order of appearance)

Stage directions (in parentheses) to explain setting, props, movements of characters as needed.

Dialogue between characters interrupted as needed by stage directions.

Individual or Group

The Jobs in Play Production

Lecture, lead group discussion, or provide written material about the following:

1. Acting:
   a. Portraying a character
   b. Speaking
   c. Moving
   d. Other
2. Directing:
   a. Learning the play
   b. Tryouts
   c. Rehearsals
   d. Dress rehearsal
3. Assistants to the director:
   a. Stage manager
   b. Prompter(s)
4. Costumes:
   a. Sources
   b. Costume designer
   c. Costume crew
5. Makeup:
   a. Reasons
   b. Kinds
   c. Makeup crew
6. Sets:
   a. Purposes
   b. Set designer
   c. Set crew
   d. Kinds of
7. Lighting:
   a. Uses
   b. Extras
   c. Cautions
8. Props:
   a. Property manager
   b. Prop crew
9. Sound Effects:
   a. Uses
   b. Sources

10. Music: (if appropriate)
    a. Kinds
    b. Cautions

Evaluation / Quiz

I. Matching: Select the best letter match for each number.

1. Actor	a. Makes, borrows, or buys all props
2. Director	b. Plans all sets
3. Stage manager	c. Sketches costume for each character
4. Prompter	d. Portrays a character
5. Costume designer	e. Makes decisions / in charge of rehearsals
6. Costume crew	f. Checks on readiness of actors and workers
7. Set designer	g. In charge of props/lists them
8. Set crew	h. Puts together all sets
9. Property manager	i. Finds or makes clothes for actors
10. Prop crew	j. Follows script during rehearsals/performances

II. True or false? Indicate T or F for each statement.

1. A cue is the last line spoken in each scene.
2. The director selects each actor to play each role.
3. Makeup is used only to suggest things about a character.
4. A set forms the background for a play.
5. Stage lighting is useful for clear vision and special effects.

Quiz Answers:

I.

1. d	2. e	3. f	4. j	5. c
6. i	7. b	8. h	9. g	10. a

II.

1. F	2. T	3. F	4. T	5. T

Dramatic Action

Lecture, lead group discussion, or provide written material to relate this information concerning the basic movement of the plot of any given play. An application of the information could be the presentation of short scenes which illustrate the movement (an example is provided).

Static situation: Protagonist on the scene facing no conflict or goal

Rising action: Protagonist finds a goal but is hampered in achieving it due to opposition by the antagonist (a series of conflicts between the protagonist and antagonists increase in intensity until the climax).

Climax: The protagonist either succeeds or fails in achieving his goal, thus ending the conflict.

Falling action: Loose ends are tied up/no goal or conflict.

Example:

Static situation: Door-to-door salesman has no customer.

Rising action: Salesman sees customer and attempts to make a sale. Customer opposes purchase. Series of conflicts occur as salesman persists and customer refuses.

Climax: Salesman is mad and threatens customer who finally buys.

Falling action: Salesman departs happy to have made a sale. There are no new prospects in sight.

Group

Create a Scene

Directions: Prepare a handout with a series of directions and space for a written response under each (see example below).

Participants will each have a pen/pencil and be seated in a circle.

Each person will write a response to the first direction on the page, initial his response, and then pass the page to the next person when directed. Then each person will read the response to #1 and respond to #2, initialing what he has written. Papers will circulate until completed or time is up. Then they will be returned to their original owners for reading, editing, and evaluation. The results can be discussed, presented, and/or read as desired.

Notes: Observe the students as they write their responses, and when most have finished call "pass." It is not necessary or desirable to wait for all responses to be completed before the pages are passed.

It is very important that each participant identify his responses. While it is OK to get silly, there can be a tendency to get inappropriate if identification is not required. If this does happen, participants can get offended, and the situation can become uncomfortable.

Sample Rotating Page

Directions: This page will be circulated when the group leader says pass. You will read prior responses and then respond to the next available item in the time provided. It is not necessary to finish each response. Please initial each entry you make, and pass when instructed to do so, finished or not. You are also cautioned to keep all remarks appropriate at all times.

1. Name and describe a character.
2. Identify and describe a place.
3. Identify a specific time period.
4. Tell what the above character is thinking.
5. Name and describe a second character who enters the scene.
6. Tell what character #2 says to #1 upon entering.
7. Tell what character #1 says back.
8. Identify an object which character #2 takes from his pocket and hands to #1.
9. Describe #1's reaction to this object.
10. Tell what happens which makes one of the characters leave the scene.
11. Provide an ending to the scene for the remaining character.

Notes: The series of response/directions can be expanded to add other characters, changes in the setting, weather, etc.

If the original person edits the resulting scene, it can be cast from among the participants and performed (perhaps the originator can do the casting and directing).

Chapter 10
Evaluation, Assessment, and Rewards

There are three basic categories of evaluation:

Daily:
- Offer frequent but sincere verbal praise and encouragement to your participants.
- Require (encourage) polite applause after each performance (no matter how short or long, good or bad).
- Refuse to permit any put-downs, negative comments, or inappropriate laughter from anyone.
- Constantly reshuffle pairings and groupings, almost never allowing participants to choose with whom they will work.
- Post an appropriate objective for each session and allow adequate time at the end for written or verbal follow up to reinforce what was accomplished and allow each participant to consider his personal achievement.

Periodic:
- Use peer- and self-evaluations and encourage discussion of the results.
- Use written evaluation forms (see a sample later in this chapter).
- Invite an audience to view performances and provide positive feedback.

End of Course:
- Require a written (and/or verbal) exam that calls on each participant to draw upon activities and experiences that he was involved in during the course/series of sessions (see a sample later in this chapter).
- Require a performance exam that calls on each participant to display the creativity and skills that he acquired or improved during the course/sessions.
- Invite an audience to view performances and to (perhaps) select a "best performance" for some award or acknowledgment.
- Poll the group to find out which performer or performance stands out as best overall during the course.

Evaluations

The following can be used as tests or more challenging activities.

Test/Challenge #1

Students respond in writing to the following prompts:

1. Describe an activity in which you participated this year and evaluate your performance.
2. Identify a familiar song. Write down the title and then …
    a. Describe the setting you would create to act it out.
    b. What would you do to act out the song? What class members would participate? How?
3. If you could play a part in any TV show, what show would it be, and what part would you play? How would you change the characterization to make it your own?
4. If you were given a bed sheet and told to plan a scene around it, what would the scene be about?
5. If you had to give a monologue from the perspective of an unborn child, what would you wear and say?
6. If you had to direct a scene which took place in the future or the past, what time period would you select and what would occur in the scene?

Test/Challenge #2

Students respond in writing to the following:

1. Describe a performance which you observed in class. Evaluate it.
2. Think of an excellent movie which you have seen. Give its title, why you selected it, and what made it special. Be specific.
3. If you could cast a part in any movie with a member of this group, who would you cast, in what part, and why?
4. If you were given a _____, and asked to plan a scene around it, what would it be like? (fill in the blank with any object, such as pacifier, beach ball, etc.)
5. If you had to give a monologue from the perspective of a person locked in a dark closet, what would you say?
6. To which person in this class would you give the Best Overall Drama Award and why?

Test/Challenge #3

Students respond in writing to the following:

1. Given the use of several folding chairs and classroom desks, describe how you would set up a scene taking place in the family kitchen. You might provide a diagram to illustrate your written description.

2. If you were to play the part of someone elderly and ill, what specific items of costume, makeup, props, etc. would you employ? How else would you convey the character?

3. One of the hardest parts of group work is organization. If you were grouped with four members of this class and told to do a scene reflecting strong emotion, what would the scene be about and who would play each part?

Project Evaluation

Students respond in writing to the following:

Sample Evaluation Sheet:

Rate the presentation of each of your classmates in each of the following categories. Rating system: A = excellent, B = good, C = fair, D = needs improvement. Be prepared to defend your comments with examples!

Performer's name: _____

Type of presentation: _____

Rate the following:

Originality: _____

Volume: _____

Poise: _____

Effort: _____

Overall: _____

Chapter 11
Grab Bag —
Miscellaneous Scene Topics

Use these scene topics whenever you have extra time to fill. Create a focus that suits you, or use them to inspire other lists of your own.

Group #1
Children abuse and mistreat another child until it becomes apparent that he has special powers.

Because of a nuclear threat, a person decides to go underground only to be hassled by others seeking safety.

Twins separated at birth are accidentally united.

A person who does not believe in ghosts is gradually convinced due to unusual occurrences.

Estranged husband/wife or good friends who had drifted apart are brought back together.

Group #2
Nasty person in the park tries to convince little kids that he is their friend.

Lead singer in a band loses his voice and others fight over the part.

Beauty pageant contestants protest that the competition should be co-ed.

Pie-eating contest at a fair gets out of hand.

A quack doctor tries to convince patients that he is for real.

Undercover cop has trouble convincing civilians that he is one of them.

Group #3
High school overnight field trip turns into a disaster.

Person admitted to the hospital finds out that he is in the mental ward.

Group of elderly patients in a nursing home decide to make life there more lively.

Group of expectant mothers are sharing pains in the pre-delivery room.

Group #4

Getting rid of something (dead body, evidence, unwanted trash, etc.)

Some moment of indecision (wedding, suicide, robbery, etc.)

Getting out of something (deep hole, doing chores, tight clothing, etc.)

Wanting the same thing that someone else has (boy/girlfriend, money, fancy car, etc.)

Getting rid of someone (wife/husband, annoying child, nosy neighbor, etc.)

Group #5

In Alaska, contrasts between activities of natives and tourists provide interest.

On a cruise ship, captain heads investigation for dangerous criminal on board.

On a ship in a storm, bad weather has made many people sick and the ship doctor has trouble coping.

Group #6

Social worker attempts to help potential dropout.

On opposite day, students become teachers.

Son/daughter refuses to go to church as expected.

Parent is upset that son/daughter is dating someone of a different religion.

Young person attempts to win a school election.

A great American is revealed to be not so great.

Person attempts to join a social club for which he is not suited.

Person accidentally travels back in time and has trouble returning.

Inventor makes a dramatic discovery only to have it stolen.

Teachers in school are replaced by robots.

Because of an accident, all human beings become machines.

Mad scientist attempts to experiment with humans without their consent.

Small insects talk about humans who threatened their existence.

Group #7

In a pet shop, a small child demands a pet from his parents.

A group of pregnant women discuss their approaching deliveries.

A girl goes to a beauty school for a perm and is surprised by the results.

An undercover cop infiltrates a high school.

A new kid arrives in an already overcrowded foster home.

A shopper notices something odd in a display but cannot convince anyone that something is afoot.

Group #8

Parents decide to divorce and have to tell the kids.

Several students disagree and others get involved.

A group of people who all want a promotion try to impress the boss.

Small children are left to play by themselves while parents visit.

It is someone's first visit to a meeting of recovering alcoholics.

A casting director goes to the streets looking for someone who is perfect for a particular part.

Several door-to-door salespeople arrive at the same house at the same time.

One of the younger members of a family gets stuck making dinner for everyone.

Group #9

A game show is set in a family living room and pits family members against one another for prizes.

A salesperson initially gets a cool reception at the home of a customer, but that soon changes.

Campers arrive excitedly at the campsite only for the weather to turn nasty.

An interior decorator arrives at the home of a client with unusual ideas for its decor.

Young people encounter resistance when they attempt to rent an apartment.

Group #10

A mental patient fools the doctor into thinking that he is sane.

Trouble starts when someone has too many drinks and annoys others in a bar.

People in an office building try to talk a jumper in off the window ledge.

Contestants on a quiz show get angry about the prizes they win.

A sale of used clothing attracts a variety of people.

Underage customers have gotten into a bar illegally.

A religious cult holds a ceremony to welcome a new member.

A group of elderly folks go on a senior citizen outing.

An argument erupts between rival street gangs.

An opera is underway when a fire breaks out, but the show must go on.

A country square dance is invaded by city slickers.

Group #11

A TV news reporter is live at the site of a disaster.

Things go very wrong for a young babysitter.

A new student is not welcome at school.

The first day on the job proves a disaster.

A young person has trouble on his first solo drive in a car.

Group #12

A person is locked up for driving drunk and decides he doesn't like the experience.

A little child runs away from home and is befriended by street people who teach him to survive.

An elderly person is so surprised at being given a surprise party that …

A child learns a lesson the hard way after disobeying his parents.

A housewife who is tired of waiting on her family goes on strike.

A woman who desperately wants children offers to baby-sit six kids, an experience which causes her to reconsider how badly she wants children of her own.

An actor/actress who is out of work is discovered by an agent while washing dishes in a restaurant.

A young person agrees to go to a late-night movie but is not prepared for what happens.

An elder sibling takes younger ones to the amusement park for the first time.

Group #13

An important client is invited to your house for dinner and you have to overlook his poor manners to get his business.

A middle-aged person seeks to stay young forever (at any cost).

Truck drivers are required to submit to blood tests to determine use of drugs/alcohol.

You have to politely tell someone you just met that you cannot associate with them.

An intelligent college student finds out that his roommate is stupid.

You demonstrate your range of emotions as you try out for a part in a play or movie.

Group #14

A little child terrified to go to the doctor is won over by office personnel.

A kid who has been in trouble at school gets help from several sources.

After an accident, a person wakes up in a hospital under treatment.

A person having adjustment problems seeks out new friends, a new job, etc.

Among friends a person begins to suspect he has mental problems.

A real estate agent shows a house with a suspicious background.

A variety of cars in a used-car lot argue over which is best.

After a long wait in a long line, the crowd gets angry when the store runs out of merchandise.

While in a fun house kids are frightened by real things.

Gangsters argue over turf to a surprise ending.

A young person is starving to death because no work is available and he won't ask for help.

A crippled person in a wheelchair watches helplessly until ...

Students are so tired that they are unable to concentrate on an important class.

While playing, kids accidentally break a window in a neighbor's house and are afraid to try to get the ball back.

Students in a science lab try to discover new formulas.

A family hurries to pack for a sudden vacation.

A customer tries to return a defective item, but various workers refuse to believe that anything is wrong.

Escaped prisoners stop for gas, and the station attendant is old and slow.

Family members are in a car having an argument when they run out of gas.

Passengers on an airplane discover that they are sitting near a famous person.

Several people who don't know one another are forced to share lodgings on jury duty.

A landlord refuses to repair/improve conditions in a house that he has rented to a family.

Group #15

During a disaster a hero emerges from the crowd.

A terrorist attempts to threaten the wrong person.

An artist has to select a model from several sources.

A disk jockey gets criticism for his music selections.

A janitor is fed up with dealing with other people's messes.

Group #16

A shy teen attempts to ask someone to dance.

A baby is stolen from the maternity ward in a hospital.

An unexpected sale is announced to customers in a store and ...

A surprise party is planned, but something goes wrong.

A new student in school is bullied.

A magician goofs up during his act.

An announcer panics when an expected guest fails to appear.

Group #17

Astronauts on a trip to Mars find out that they don't have enough fuel to return home.

Several novices go on a hot-air balloon ride.

Window-washers (new at the job) are working on the 17th floor.

After excessive bragging, a "sports expert" is challenged to play and ...

After coming home late from a date, a teenager invites his companion in and a grandparent is awakened.

Several people who plan to room together disagree on how to decorate/arrange the apartment.

Group #18

Teens in stress

Recycling campaign

Starting own business

Functioning on too little sleep

Parking lot squabble

Rumors hurt

A band reunion

A fashion show

Shopping for the prom

photo by Bob Betlow

About the Author

Lynda Topper was a teacher of English on the High School level for 29 years in the Baltimore City and Baltimore County, Maryland, Public School Systems. For ten of those years she also taught two elective courses in Theatre Arts and directed the extracurricular student plays and five faculty productions. These are the years she had the good fortune to work with many enthusiastic students and faculty members who provided the experience and inspiration for this book.

Lynda was born in Baltimore City and grew up in the Hamilton area. After receiving her Bachelor of Science degree in Secondary Education with a major in English from Towson State College, she began her teaching career. Taking courses at night and in the summer, she earned her Masters Degree in Secondary Education.

Now retired, she spends her time reading, traveling, swimming, and enjoying nature. Living in a Northern suburb of Maryland with her husband, she is currently working on her second book that is a practical guide to planning and enjoying overnight excursions to New York City. This work, as was the first, is based on over twenty years of personal experience in doing just that.

Order Form

Meriwether Publishing Ltd.
PO Box 7710
Colorado Springs, CO 80933-7710
Phone: 800-937-5297 Fax: 719-594-9916
Website: www.meriwether.com

Please send me the following books:

_____ **Theatre Games and Activities #BK-B304** **$17.95**
by Lynda A. Topper
Games for building confidence and creativity

_____ **Theatre Games for Young Performers** **$17.95**
#BK-B188
by Maria C. Novelly
Improvisations and exercises for developing acting skills

_____ **More Theatre Games for** **$17.95**
Young Performers #BK-268
by Suzi Zimmerman
Improvisations and exercises for developing acting skills

_____ **Theatre Games and Beyond #BK-B217** **$17.95**
by Amiel Schotz
A creative approach for performers

_____ **Acting Games #BK-B168** **$17.95**
by Marsh Cassady
A textbook of theatre games and improvisations

_____ **Improv Ideas #BK-B283** **$22.95**
by Justine Jones and Mary Ann Kelley
A book of games and lists

_____ **112 Acting Games #BK-B277** **$17.95**
by Gavin Levy
A comprehensive workbook of theatre games

**These and other fine Meriwether Publishing books are available at
your local bookstore or direct from the publisher. Prices subject to
change without notice. Check our website or call for current prices.**

Name: _____ e-mail: _____

Organization name: _____

Address: _____

City: _____ State: _____

Zip: _____ Phone: _____

❑ **Check enclosed**

❑ **Visa / MasterCard / Discover / Am. Express #** _____

Signature: _____   *Expiration
date:* _____ / _____
        (required for credit card orders)

Colorado residents: Please add 3% sales tax.
Shipping: Include $3.95 for the first book and 75¢ for each additional book ordered.

❑ *Please send me a copy of your complete catalog of books and plays.*

Order Form

Meriwether Publishing Ltd.
PO Box 7710
Colorado Springs, CO 80933-7710
Phone: 800-937-5297 Fax: 719-594-9916
Website: www.meriwether.com

Please send me the following books:

_____ **Theatre Games and Activities #BK-B304** **$17.95**
by Lynda A. Topper
Games for building confidence and creativity

_____ **Theatre Games for Young Performers** **$17.95**
#BK-B188
by Maria C. Novelly
Improvisations and exercises for developing acting skills

_____ **More Theatre Games for** **$17.95**
Young Performers #BK-268
by Suzi Zimmerman
Improvisations and exercises for developing acting skills

_____ **Theatre Games and Beyond #BK-B217** **$17.95**
by Amiel Schotz
A creative approach for performers

_____ **Acting Games #BK-B168** **$17.95**
by Marsh Cassady
A textbook of theatre games and improvisations

_____ **Improv Ideas #BK-B283** **$22.95**
by Justine Jones and Mary Ann Kelley
A book of games and lists

_____ **112 Acting Games #BK-B277** **$17.95**
by Gavin Levy
A comprehensive workbook of theatre games

These and other fine Meriwether Publishing books are available at your local bookstore or direct from the publisher. Prices subject to change without notice. Check our website or call for current prices.

Name: _____ e-mail: _____

Organization name: _____

Address: _____

City: _____ State: _____

Zip: _____ Phone: _____

❑ **Check enclosed**

❑ **Visa / MasterCard / Discover / Am. Express #** _____

Expiration
Signature: _____ date: _____ / _____
          (required for credit card orders)

Colorado residents: Please add 3% sales tax.
Shipping: Include $3.95 for the first book and 75¢ for each additional book ordered.

❑ *Please send me a copy of your complete catalog of books and plays.*